CREATING & DELIVERING WINNING

ADVERTISING & MARKETING PRESENTATIONS

Second Edition

SANDRA MORIARTY   TOM DUNCAN

NTC Business Books
NTC/Contemporary Publishing Group

Library of Congress Cataloging-in-Publication Data

Moriarty, Sandra E. (Sandra Ernst)
    Creating & delivering winning advertising & marketing
presentations / Sandra Moriarty, Tom Duncan.
      p.   cm.
    Rev. ed. of: How to create and deliver winning advertising
presentations. c1989.
    Includes index.
    ISBN 0-8442-3529-6
    1. Sales presentations—Handbooks, manuals, etc.   2. Advertising—
Handbooks, manuals, etc.   I. Duncan, Tom (Thomas R.)
II. Moriarty, Sandra E. (Sandra Ernst). How to create and deliver
winning advertising presentations.   III. Title.   IV. Title: Creating
and delivering winning advertising and marketing presentations.
HF5438.8.P7M67   1995
658.8′101—dc20   94-30848
                                          CIP

1996 Printing

Published by NTC Business Books, a division of NTC Publishing Group
4255 West Touhy Avenue
Lincolnwood (Chicago), Illinois 60646-1975, U.S.A.
© 1995 by NTC Publishing Group. All rights reserved.
No part of this book may be reproduced, stored in a retrieval system,
or transmitted in any form or by any means,
electronic, mechanical, photocopying, recording or otherwise,
without the prior permission of NTC Publishing Group.
Manufactured in the United States of America.

8 9 ML 9 8 7 6 5 4 3 2

CONTENTS

SECTION II

PRODUCING THE PRESENTATION

SECTION III

GIVING THE PRESENTATION

The What, How, and Why of Business Presentations

One month after Joseph Nacchio took over as head of the AT&T consumer division in 1993, he wanted an advertising agency review. Five agencies shared AT&T's business: N. W. Ayer, Young & Rubicam, Ogilvy & Mather, McCann-Erickson, and Foote, Cone & Belding.

One week after letters of inquiry were sent out, Dick Martin, AT&T vice president of corporate communications, met with a top representative of each agency. The ground rules were established. The agencies would be briefed at the same meeting, each agency could decide for itself how many people to bring to the final presentation, and AT&T would compensate them for out-of-pocket expenses.

At the briefing, each agency was asked to sign a non-disclosure form and then given proprietary information. They had one month to develop an advertising strategy, a creative strategy, and samples of creative executions. A committee of nine from AT&T would listen to the presentations and score the results. Presenting order was drawn by lot.

When the month was up, the first agency to present was Young & Rubicam. The AT&T team went to the agency's offices and heard a presentation from CEO Alex Kroll, who had a long track record working on the account, and other Y&R staff. The agency's relationship with AT&T was good enough for it to retain its current billings, but the presentation, which included a produced commercial, wasn't strong enough to win new business.

That afternoon the AT&T review group visited McCann. The agency used storyboards rather than a finished commercial and that hurt it.

According to an executive familiar with the presentation, "If McCann had done 10% better in its creative presentation, the agency stood a good chance to win the business."

The next morning the AT&T group went to Ogilvy & Mather. The verbal presentation was strong, stronger in fact than the creative ideas, and that cost the agency the account.

Later that day the AT&T group visited Ayer, which, like Y&R, had also prepared a commercial. While the commercial was a relatively low cost and in-house production, it helped and the chemistry between the two groups during the presentation was good.

The next day saw the group at FC&B's offices. The agency was considered a long shot since it had handled less AT&T business than the others. But FC&B saw this as an advantage and positioned itself as an outsider. It felt that the recent shifts in AT&T management might indicate a willingness to try new approaches. Rather than getting bogged down in telecommunications technology, FC&B focused on common sense strategic thinking. It also came prepared to address AT&T's main competition, MCI.

For three days following the agency presentations, the AT&T group met to discuss what they were looking for in an agency. Then each member of the AT&T review team graded each agency in terms of market assessment, media and research approaches, creative thinking, and plans to win over competitors' customers.

The results: FC&B was unanimously picked the winner, Ayer was second, and Y&R third. Although the content of the presentation was the critical factor, how information was packaged in the live presentations was a key factor in the AT&T decision.

What Is a Presentation?

A presentation is an oral delivery supported by visuals and audio media that reinforce and in some cases carry the bulk of the message. The content of the message is a set of recommendations accompanied by all the persuasion that logic and argument can bring to the message. A written plansbook may also be prepared to leave behind, but its function is more to document the details of the proposal than it is to persuade. While oral delivery may not be as efficient as a written document, it is used in business because a personal presentation has more impact and intensity than a written one. Although most presentations are accompanied by a written proposal or plansbook, the presentation is important because it allows the presenters to have more control over the audience's perception of a message. Furthermore, because of the immediate feedback, the audience's objections, questions, and concerns can be immediately addressed.

Who Makes Presentations?

Regardless of role or title, nearly everyone makes oral presentations at some time or another. Sooner or later, you will, too. Presentations are made by people working in every area of marketing. When IBM approaches AT&T for new business, it uses a presentation. IBM is the supplier; AT&T is the prospective client, or prospect. In particular, all areas of marketing communication—advertising, public relations, sales promotion, direct response, even packaging—have professionals who make new business presentations to clients or prospects. Presentation skills are needed in every area of marketing and marketing communication.

How can you learn to be a winning presenter? While it may be some time before you will be presenting for a $50 million account, you can still practice and improve your individual presentation skills. You may begin by participating in in-house presentations for bosses or colleagues. The more experienced and effective a presenter you become, the more often you will be asked to make presentations to outsiders.

This book packages many people's experiences and summarizes and confirms what presentation professionals have learned from many years of winning and losing presentations. It is directed to you as an individual as well as a member of a team. Whether you are working alone or with others, the time you spend on your feet, however, is yours alone. Your success is a product of your own presence, style, organization, and presentation skills. Even when you are on a team that loses, you may still win because your own presentation was outstanding and caught the attention of important people.

Importance of Presentation Skills

People who are good speakers and presenters become important, even powerful, because of that skill. Thomas Leech, in his book on presentations, points out that for many professionals "oral communication is a continuous requirement. . . . Any professional who wants to have as great an influence as possible recognizes that professional skills go hand in hand with communication skills."

There's an adage that most executives spend 70 percent of their time in meetings. What are they doing in meetings? Most often they are listening to presentations. Any time one staff member has a proposal to make to someone else, presentation is involved. Situations must be explained, problems outlined, solutions identified, and approaches justified. Whether it is one-on-one at a desk, one person talking to a group of 15 around a conference table, or several people speaking to 150 at a dealers' meeting, presentation skills are essential if business is to be successfully conducted. Most managers and executives make oral presentations weekly or even daily.

Leonard Meuse, Jr., in his book on presentations, explains why presentations are so important. An informal or working presentation generates immediate feedback from key people. In addition, a presentation has an impact that written reports lack. You can create a sense of immediacy with a presentation that demands some kind of response. Written reports can get shuffled, forgotten, or lost.

Business is run by committees and committees involve one or more people trying to explain their ideas to one or more listeners. The listeners, in turn, may become presenters as they try to explain their views and reactions. "Communicator power" determines the direction that business takes.

COMMUNICATOR POWER

People who present themselves well have an advantage in the office, in the conference room, and in the meeting hall. New business, as well as more business, goes to people who can present their ideas convincingly. This book will give you that edge, that advantage that lets you be the winner.

Control

One thing that sings through most people's experience, and is a central point in this book, is that presentations are interactive. You are not just giving a speech, you are talking with someone, no matter how large the audience. A presentation is a structured conversation. You want the attention, the understanding, and the feedback of your audience.

A good presenter is a step ahead of the audience and totally in control of its attention. Those in the audience, be they clients, bosses, or salespeople, are continually thinking. What they are thinking about, to a large extent, depends on you and what you are presenting. You can direct their thinking with the right presentation skills.

Control of audience attention comes through planning. You want control over every element that could affect the perception and understanding of your message. That includes message design, setting, seating, casting, AV media, and, of course, the actual delivery.

To control their attention, your presentation must be as well planned as a good business plan. Designing a presentation is like designing an effective ad. You must know the target and what they are like (attitudes, wants, needs), show how your idea can benefit them, why they should believe your promises, and what they need to do (your recommended action) to get the promised benefit.

Persuasion

Control over the situation is also gained by a mesmerizing and persuasive performance. Presentations are performances where speakers are trying to sell something—the company, the company's ideas for a project, a change in direction or budgetary allocations, research findings, a supplier's services, and so on. The stakes determine how large a production the presentation will be. Presentations can involve dozens of staff, thousands of dollars, and months of work.

Selling yourself and your ideas is an important part of any presentation, but the real challenge is to make it interesting. Tom Hagan, who has worked with a number of major agencies and has been co-chairman of Denver-based Karsh & Hagan, Inc., says, "We've been told by clients and prospects that most of the agency presentations they've been subjected to are similar. Most are boring. Most take too much time talking about the agency and about things that are already known to everyone in the room."

This book is dedicated to helping you prepare presentations that are persuasive, entertaining, and on target, so your prospects will not report that they have just been "subjected to" a boring presentation.

THE PRESENTATION PROCESS

This book will lead you through the process of developing a presentation. The chapters follow this process, which is illustrated in figure 1.

Section I is about planning activities and is structured around three topics:

1. *The strategy* includes knowing the audience and understanding the purpose and objective of the presentation.

2. *The message* focuses on message organization, persuasive elements, and scripting and editing.

3. *The audiovisual media* looks at the various types of AV media used in presentations and at the functions of visuals in presenting the message.

Section II looks at the *production of the presentation*, in the sense that a director looks at the production of a play or commercial. There are two central topics in this section:

4. *Designing and producing the visuals* focuses on production techniques for visuals in general as well as production techniques for specific types of visuals.

5. *Orchestrating the presentation* focuses on the details and arrangements involved in making the presentation.

Section III focuses on *making the presentation* itself. There are three chapters:

6. *Making the presentation* deals with setting up the room, presenters' styles and credibility, reading the audience, and handling the mechanics of equipment and visuals.

7. *Delivering your message* looks at individual presentation styles and delivery techniques.

8. *Presentation follow-up* looks at the end of the presentation and what happens afterwards.

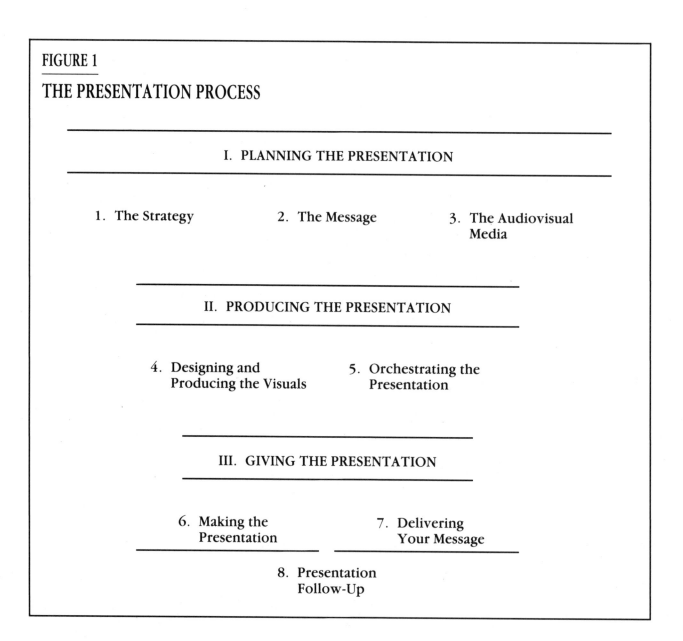

FIGURE 1

THE PRESENTATION PROCESS

I. PLANNING THE PRESENTATION

1. The Strategy   2. The Message   3. The Audiovisual
                                                       Media

II. PRODUCING THE PRESENTATION

4. Designing and   5. Orchestrating the
   Producing the Visuals   Presentation

III. GIVING THE PRESENTATION

6. Making the   7. Delivering
   Presentation   Your Message

8. Presentation
   Follow-Up

SECTION I

PLANNING THE PRESENTATION

CHAPTER 1

Presentation Strategy

KEY POINTS
✎ Presentation strategy varies with the situation
✎ The more formal the presentation, the more preparation needed
✎ Know your assignment
✎ Know your prospective audience like you know your target
✎ Speak to your audience's point of view
✎ Your audience isn't your adversary
✎ Anticipate objections

How you approach the planning of a presentation depends upon your strategy, your audience, and what you want to accomplish. The type of presentation and the scale of its production varies with the dollars at stake and the kind of decision being made. Different types of presentation situations call for different types of strategy.

Different presentation situations also call for different message strategies. All types of presentations, however, use some similar techniques. For example, almost all are supported by skillful use of visual media such as slides, flip charts, overheads, or presentation boards. Almost all require delivery skills similar to those you may have studied in a speech course. Finally, there is usually some kind of leave-behind printed material. It may be as informal as a memo or as sophisticated as a full-blown plansbook.

Types of Presentations

SALES PRESENTATIONS

Sales presentations can be formal or informal. They are usually made one on one or in small group sessions. Some are requested by potential customers and some are cold calls, where sales representatives drop in unannounced. Some sales presentations are tailored for individual clients. Some are more generic in nature. In order to offer both consistency and flexibility, a number of companies are preparing a menu of presentations that can be used by sales reps in a wide variety of situations. Portable interactive media devices are allowing reps to take a huge library of different prerecorded presentation materials with them and pull up those that apply to specific needs.

Every quarter Apple Computer sends 5,000 of its employees a two-CD set of 150 presentations. Ninety percent of those employees use them five or more times a month and make 3.5 times more sales calls per month while saving 11 hours per month over those who do not use them. According to David Grabel, manager of Apple USA sales communications, ''We've been able to create a totally automated process. There's only one person who collects, organizes and manages the system.''

CLIENT PRESENTATIONS

Campaign and Project Presentations

Companies that are currently working for clients need to periodically update clients on their efforts. The participants are known and the presentation builds on previous experiences. Sometimes these presentations are merely new executions of the current projects. At other times they may involve the introduction of an entirely new idea or direction. These presentations may be formal or they may be more like a ''work session.'' Either way, they begin with a foundation of basic information but move quickly to persuasion. The purpose of these presentations is to convince the client that the soliciting company's solution to the current problem is sound, even brilliant. Presenters are trying to convince an oftentimes skeptical critic, a critic who ultimately has the power of life and death over the account as well as over the participants' jobs.

New Business Presentations

New business or speculative presentations are more formal and often intense. These are made in a competitive environment where the client has invited a number of outside firms or agencies to compete for the account, as in the AT&T story reported in the Introduction. Often called shootouts, these "spec" presentations build the reputations of the presenting companies by demonstrating their skills and expertise. New business presentations can be costly, and they demand the best presenters and work the agency has available. The costs for new business presentations can range from $1,000 to $250,000. Some have even reached as high as $500,000. In some cases the client may partially underwrite out-of-pocket expenses, but seldom do they contribute enough to cover all the staff time and production expenses.

New business presentations are often more formal and polished than campaign presentations simply because the stakes are higher. The spec presentation approach is also used in a review situation where the client is deciding whether to retain the current consulting firm or agency or hire a new firm or agency.

A new business presentation should begin by introducing your company. To do this, answer these questions about your company: Who are you? What can you do? and What have you done in the past? If you have any areas of specialty, point them out and build on them.

Spec presentations should not focus too much on old accounts. Successful new business presenters recommend that the focus be kept on what your company can do for the account you are pitching. Use recent past work, not as a history lesson, but as case studies that document your problem-solving abilities. For example, you might want to say you have knowledge of the product, product category, problem, or target audience in question. You can justify your knowledge by referring to some similar situation you successfully handled on another one of your accounts. The more current your case histories are, the more meaningful they will be.

Other information that might be covered includes staff and team membership. Because of the high stakes, new business presentations are often made by people who specialize in presenting frequently to the principals of the company. The client wants to know who they will be working with, so introduce and, better yet, involve the people who will be assigned to the account. Often clients complain that the soliciting company's top brass give the impression they'll be running the account. Instead, all the client sees for the next six months are young, inexperienced new staff. To avoid creating mistrust, the top brass should make it clear they will not be involved in day-to-day contact but will be working behind the scenes at the agency.

You may also want to include some comments about your track record with past accounts. If your company has a good record of retaining accounts and keeping them happy, say so.

One caution from John Grant, an experienced ad executive, is that new business presentations can be dangerous because the soliciting company is typically operating without a solid information base. He notes, "It's easy to misinterpret goals, needs, and budget and come in way out in the blue. You may not understand where the company is financially because that information isn't available to you." Be cautious and don't assume too much.

Use past work as a case study and apply it to this situation

SCALE OF THE PRESENTATION

> The more formal the presentation, the more preparation needed

Presentations range in scale from informal one-on-one talks to formal extravaganzas where you are presenting to an auditorium full of clients, stockholders, franchisees, or salespeople. Formality in presentations generally depends on the size of the audience. The bigger it is, the more formal the presentation.

The level of formality is also a function of the action needed. The more significant the decision, the more formal the presentation tends to be. A simple update tends to be more casual, more like a shirt-sleeves working session. Without exception, the more formal the presentation, the more preparation time needed.

INFORMAL MINI-PRESENTATION

Mini-presentations are held daily within a company to allow staff members to present new ideas and results of meetings or planning sessions with accounts or customers. They may be as simple as one person talking out a plan with a co-worker, or a meeting called to update other staff on the progress of a project. The purpose of these informal, small-group sessions is explanation and/or persuasion. They are in-house sessions and the audience is a group of colleagues. An account executive, for example, may present the results of a client meeting to the rest of the account team; primarily they serve an informational function.

Persuasion is needed when you are recommending a new business plan, creative strategy, research project, package design, or promotion proposal. The problem is presented, alternatives weeded out, the approach discussed, and feedback requested. Informal presentations to the client during campaign development may involve both explanation and persuasion.

SEMI-FORMAL, SMALL-GROUP PRESENTATION

This is the most common situation for presentations and a major focus of this book.

These presentations are much more serious and involved than staff presentations. Here, a new plan in its entirety is presented officially to a management committee and then to the customer or client. New business presentations also fit this same category, although they may be even more polished. A proposal presentation is a formal situation that may involve a small or medium-sized audience watching a presentation by a number of company people who are assigned specific roles.

FORMAL, LARGE-GROUP PRESENTATION

After a major proposal has been accepted, the company may be asked to make its presentation to the distributors, dealers, or salespeople. Because this often occurs at a convention, large-group presentation techniques are necessary. This might involve working in an auditorium, wearing a microphone, and being blinded by stage lights. The strategy is to focus on the performance aspects of the presentation, which must be entertaining, even mesmerizing.

FORMAL ONE-ON-ONE PRESENTATION

One last type of presentation is equally serious, but usually made to an audience of only one or two: the everyday sales presentation. The message may be formal and scripted, accompanied by a set of prepared visuals, or it may be delivered in a more casual form as a conversation.

CROSS-CULTURAL PRESENTATION

As the world market expands many businesses must communicate internationally. An international presentation poses several unique problems. The most obvious barrier is language. Although many international business people outside of the U.S. speak English as either their second or third language, variations in dialect and speed may make communication difficult. Translators can be helpful but tough to coordinate. Try to find quality translators that can translate the material simultaneously with your presentation.

Be sure to start your presentation slowly and to speak clearly. Give the audience time to understand and absorb your message. Smile during your presentation—a smile is language. Visuals will ease the discussion of numbers and comparisons and a pointer is a great tool to help your audience follow along.

Finally, and perhaps the most difficult task involved in making an international presentation, you must research the customs and traditions of your audience. Remember many jokes and sayings either cannot be translated into another language, or may lose (or add) something critical in the translation!

UNDERSTANDING THE ASSIGNMENT

Early in the planning you and your team should meet representatives of the department, company, or agency requesting the presentation. What do they have in mind? What do they want from you? Are they launching a new product or repositioning an old one? This initial conference can help your company get a firm grasp on the assignment before any planning begins.

FERRETING OUT THE REAL PROBLEM

Finding out the real problem you have been asked to solve is a very subtle form of interpersonal research. Sometimes companies know exactly what they want to hear, but they won't tell you because they want to see if you read the situation as they do. If you don't, you better be able to justify your interpretation since it differs from theirs.

Sometimes companies are confused. They may not know which direction they want you to take. The mid-management people you are dealing with may not see the problem the same way the CEO does. William M. Claggett, in an article in *Advertising Age* on how clients view advertising pitches, described this problem: "Aside from identifying the real decision-maker, the hardest thing for agencies (and some clients themselves) to figure out is on what basis the decision will really be based." He explains that sometimes "the 'official' ground rules are drafted by junior people who are trying to record what their bosses are telling them. This usually results in carefully defined ground rules, which sometimes are not followed in the heat of the decision-making process."

Sometimes companies will tell you what they want, but you can tell, later on in the planning, that that is not what they need. They may be too close to the situation to be able to see the real problem. Then you have to develop a plan that lets you make a counter-recommendation without appearing to neglect the original assignment or request. It's tricky.

When several advertising agencies were going after the MasterCard account, they found the ground shifting beneath them. According to one executive who was getting feedback from the MasterCard committee, "The more the MasterCard executives heard, the more it shook their own beliefs about their business. They got a little vague." According to an executive from one of the agencies, "They'd say something on Thursday, and then on Friday they'd come back at you and say, 'We've thought it through further.' They seemed to have no confidence in their decisions."

LISTENING BETWEEN THE WORDS

Interpret the initial assignment carefully. Many a team has discovered with chagrin that the brilliant proposal they presented did not address the right problem. They were so mesmerized by the opportunity they saw that they missed the real problem they were supposed to solve.

Listening is the most important part of problem-solving and the most important interpersonal skill needed when preparing a presentation for a specific account problem. Listen to what clients say and to what they don't say. Just as you learn to read between the lines, you should learn to listen between the words.

KNOWING YOUR PROSPECT

A presentation is a very direct form of what communication theorists call "two-way communication." You address audience members directly, look in their eyes, read their reactions, and answer their questions on the spot. In presentation strategy, your first and most important task is to analyze your prospects so you can provide them with information they need and recommendations they will want to adopt.

RESEARCH YOUR AUDIENCE

Know your client like you know your target

The first step in audience analysis is to know to whom you are talking and that means knowing their names and their titles. It also means knowing who is responsible for making decisions and who influences the decision maker. To reach the audience effectively, profile them. This profile can begin in your orientation meeting and will become more refined as you research and develop your presentation.

EXHIBIT 1.1

KNOW YOUR AUDIENCE

To get to know your client as well as you know your target, answer these questions:

1. Who are they as individuals? As a group?
2. What do they already know? What don't they know?
3. What can you tell them that will surprise them?
4. How will they use the information you're going to give them?
5. What do they want to hear? What don't they want to hear?
6. What are their concerns? Worries?
7. What biases might get in the way?
8. Who has a stake in the outcome? What kind?
9. Who has territory to protect?
10. Who has an ax to grind?
11. Who's a friend? Who isn't? Why?

IDENTIFY THE DECISION MAKER

Skilled presenters are good at identifying the figure they call ''Mr. Big,'' the person, male or female, who has the power to say yes or no. In the article in *Advertising Age* quoted earlier, William Clagget observes, ''Curiously, it is not always the ultimate boss who makes the decisions. In large, multi-divisional situations it can be the person in charge of the brand (brand manager), the one in charge of the brand category group, the category marketing director or someone else.'' He calls this someone else ''the Owl'' and notes that ''Many an agency new business person has made a strategic error by winking and nodding to the wrong person in a new-business presentation.''

Don't just go by titles. Sometimes the real decision maker is not the highest ranking person present. For example, many corporate presidents will defer operating decisions to their department vice-presidents. It's best to find this out through preliminary research—by talking to people who know them and their organization and who have worked with them. If that information is not available, then try to pick up on it by watching the patterns of deference in play during the introductions and preliminary socializing. You may notice that it's not the person with the biggest title who appears to command the most respect. Look also for the influencers. Even ''Mr. Big'' may have an associate on whom he or she relies for advice. That person's judgment and approval may be critical.

It's a matter of ''reading'' your audience. Tony Wainwright, vice-chairman of CME in New York, tells a story about a presentation to a macaroni firm that he worked on when he was with Marschalk. ''We went all out. We visited the factory, did some original research and developed several campaigns. The top man was a solid, conservative executive. Our mistake was in providing 'too much flash' and we scared him away.'' Wainwright explains, ''Later I found out that, although he liked our thinking, he was intimidated by us and felt we were too slick.''

In another case an accounting firm was forewarned before making its new business pitch that the key decision maker was a passive listener. Knowing this presenters weren't thrown by his lack of response during the formal presentation and made the sale.

SPEAK TO THE CLIENT'S VIEW

Purpose

Speak to their point of view

Before a presentation, you should interrogate the company's representative to find out what is expected to happen as a result of the presentation. At a client orientation meeting, for example, Tom Hagan thoroughly interviews the client. ''We ask what the client knows and what they want to know. That allows us to organize our presentation so it is concise, pertinent, in-depth where it should be, and on target. It also helps us avoid traps where we might say the wrong thing.'' Interviews with staff can continue after the orientation meeting. Talk to as many people as you can without being a nuisance.

Getting accurate information about the client's viewpoint can be a problem when there are many levels of management on the client side. "We like to do business with the CEO," Hagan said, "he knows where the company is headed. If we can, we try to schedule an interview with him before making the presentation.'' Hagan says if his agency can't get access to the CEO, then they anticipate and project the client's viewpoint from the agency's analysis of the industry and marketplace.

Hagan covers the lack of client contact (or questionable client-supplied data) by starting a presentation with a restatement of the instructions given to the agency. ''We start off by playing back to the entire audience what we have been told should be the objective of the presentation. That way everyone knows why we're there.'' He explains, ''sometimes it happens that the person who requested or arranged the presentation gives us wrong, misleading, or incomplete directions. We want everyone to know where we got that 'dumb idea.' ''

Knowledge

Your presentation must speak to the client's needs, expectations, and level of knowledge. Nothing ensures this better than first-hand experience with the client's business. When D'Arcy-MacManus, Masius (now D'Arcy Masius Benton & Bowles) was making a presentation for the Budweiser account, agency people were sent to brewery school along with the wholesalers and distributors. Clark Heidtke, then an art director for Foote, Cone & Belding, found himself working in a Hallmark store prior to his agency's pitch for Hallmark Cards.

Likewise, when Campbell-Ewald was making a presentation to Nimrod for its fold-down trailers, Heidtke lived in one for a week. He brought in a model and a photo team and shot the trailer to demonstrate a variety of uses from a formal dinner to an artfully arranged collection of sporting equipment. The slides were just intended for the presentation, but some became illustrations in the final advertisements. Ad executive Charlotte Beers showed Sears she was interested in their products when she took apart and reassembled a Sears power drill while presenting her agency's marketing plan for them.

Companies, particularly on a new business pitch, don't expect an outside agency or consultant to know all about them and their business. They merely want to see some indication that preliminary research has been done. In fact, a presenter can get in trouble by pretending to be a totally knowledgeable expert in a company's business. The client wants the outside company to be an expert in its own area of specialty, not in whatever the client is selling. It is important that you let the prospect know you understand the business, but remember: they want to know how knowledgeable you are about your business and how that will benefit their marketing efforts.

Client Interest

One of the problems in presentations is figuring out what the client wants to hear. Some are interested in background research, others want to hear about strategy, and some aren't interested in anything but what it will cost. John Grant remembers one client in the cosmetics industry who operated "on guts and feelings. You could hear his fingers tapping while the numbers guys were talking about research. Finally the client said, 'where's the stuff?' " All he wanted to see was the creative.

Tom Hagan describes a similar experience. His co-chairman, Phil Karsh, was describing what Karsh & Hagan calls "the disciplines," the agency's approach to media and creative workplans, when the client interrupted Karsh to say, "Skip this discipline crap and show me some of what you've done." Karsh replied, "We don't do anything 'til we've done the disciplines." Hagan observed, "We knew we were in trouble the rest of the presentation because the big guy was quiet and pouted." He concluded, "We didn't get the business. But sometimes you find out during a presentation that you don't want the business." When IBM was looking for a new agency to handle its PC account, it told the participating agencies that they couldn't use boards, videos, or multimedia presentations. What it wanted was a discussion of strategy over lunch or dinner.

The "Me Screen"

The "Me Screen" . . . what does it mean to me?

A "Me Screen" operates in every presentation. The clients want to hear what your proposal will mean to them; furthermore they will only pay attention to what they want to hear. That may or may not be what you want them to understand.

Presenters have their own "Me Screen." They can get all wrapped up in the subtleties of their logic and the brilliance of their ideas, and miss the point of the problem. Remember, it's not your solution; it's theirs. Avoid phrases like, "Our solution is to . . ." That suggests that you have taken over management of the client's company. All you can do is recommend; you can't assume the decision making.

CLIENT RELATIONSHIPS

According to CEO Tom Hall of Chicago's Ogilvy & Mather, "A new business competition is a combination of two things: one, obviously, is the substance of what you bring to the prospect, but the other is, it's a 'chemistry' test." He explained, "one of the reasons there's a meeting is so the prospect can see if some chemistry can develop, and it's hard to fall in love with people if you only see each of them for three minutes."

Hall recommends that only a few people meet with the client. "When you bring in fewer people, and those few people cover a broader array of topics than they would otherwise, it gives those few people a chance to really show their stuff, to show that they are very well-versed and fully-rounded professionals capable of talking, discussing, or presenting a wider array of subjects than just a narrowly focused, specialized field. It gives the prospect in a new business presentation a better opportunity to develop respect for each of those individuals.''

Your company comes in from outside to solve a particular problem. The client (or prospect) may or may not like your solution. If they don't, a natural reaction for you is to be defensive. You may find yourself thinking that the client is dumb, intransigent, even reactionary, and obviously mired in the mud of past practices. Your client, on the other hand, may have turned down your proposal for any number of perfectly valid reasons which you aren't in a position to understand or appreciate. For example, the W.B. Doner ad agency thought it had solved all of Subaru of America's problems when it presented multiple campaigns to the car company. Unfortunately, instead of highlighting the agency's versatility, the presentation confused the Subaru committee. One member of the Subaru committee said Doner didn't have a focused theme demonstrating an understanding of Subaru and its needs. ''Too much of the satelliting and filming of the dealers and everything but getting to know us.''

All outside advisors have a blind spot in the client-advisor relationship because they don't know all the client's pressures and priorities. Sometimes this keeps the consultant objective and allows him or her to bring a fresh point of view. At other times, however, it makes them look naive, especially if they press for certain actions which have a low priority for the client.

Resistance Points

People turn down ideas, even good ideas, for reasons that may not seem logical. There is always a little pocket of resistance to a genuinely new idea just because it's new. Every new idea replaces an old one. A new idea assaults the client's old practices and possibly their ego and that can been as a criticism of the way they have done business in the past. Proposing a new idea takes gentleness and tact. It's best to build on the past rather than tear it down. Show how your new idea is based on something brilliant they've already done. Position it as an extension rather than a replacement. Others may turn down a good new idea because they don't understand it. Simple misunderstanding is often a factor in negative responses. Make sure the explanation is adequate to the complexities of the proposal and the knowledge level of the audience.

Don't be patronizing. If you talk over their heads, use lots of jargon or try to impress them with fancy statistics, they may say no just because you made them feel foolish. Susanne Townsend, in an *Advertising Age* article, observed that one of her smartest clients told her that she doesn't want to be made to feel dumb. Sometimes a perfectly good idea is rejected because it doesn't enhance the status of someone important, like the client's marketing manager.

Show the manager how he or she can benefit from it. Can it help that manager win respect or a promotion?

It may also be seen as a status infringement. Your new idea may step on someone's toes or move into someone else's turf. The easiest way to handle an infringement problem is to presell your idea. Talk to the most sensitive parties ahead of time to work out their objections and convince them they will benefit.

Office politics can give your great idea a bad case of indigestion and you may never know why. Sometimes people make deals that have nothing whatsoever to do with the proposal. One person supports or doesn't support an idea as a way of paying off or paying back someone else. You can get blindsided for what appears to be no reason at all.

You may run up against some personalities that can cause grief for a new idea. Superboss, for example, may be a superperfectionist. He or she will never support something unless it is perfect which, of course, is impossible given this person's standards. Mr. Twiddle, on the other hand, lacks confidence and can't make a decision. Preselling helps solve these personality problems, too. If you make sure Superboss sees everything ahead of time, you'll have time to work out whatever he or she sees as imperfections. Get Mr. Twiddle the support of a crowd so he doesn't feel out on a limb. Then he won't have to make a decision alone. Regardless of the personalities involved, preselling is a useful strategy. John Grant uses it to get the client to "buy in." He has found that then "they're not surprised or shocked. It gets them involved in developing the proposal. It also gives us time to correct any wrong approaches."

One final reason for resistance is that your idea may not be as great as you think it is. Again, this could be a result of not knowing or understanding client priorities. You should be open-minded enough to consider this possibility. Many companies are used to selling, and selling hard. Once they have an agenda, they charge ahead, completely focused on getting client approval. In their zealousness, they may take client objections too lightly.

PRESENTATION COSTS

The cost of a presentation can grow like a Pentagon budget. Some major new business presentations for big accounts have run as high as $500,000. When Foote, Cone & Belding wanted to land the Alka-Seltzer Plus account, it had more than 150 of its 475 employees involved in some way. But it did win the account. Most companies can't afford to spend that much on a speculative presentation. If they do, they have to know that the account is worth the gamble.

One of the first decisions to be made is to determine what kind of budget makes sense for the presentation. Given the size of the account, how much should you be spending? Start by estimating the staff time and production expenses for various types of presentations. What's the bottom line? Does it make sense to invest that much in this account? This management decision must be made early in the planning.

STRATEGIC PRESENTATIONS

The basis of strategic thinking is understanding the type of presentation you will be making, recognizing its purpose, and knowing what is expected of you. Audience analysis is the key to successful message design. You have to know your audience in order to know what they want, and you have to know how they see the problem in order to solve it. Plan your presentation according to the needs, values and tastes of your prospective client. Once you have a ''good read'' on your prospect, you can construct a presentation that is right on target.

CHAPTER 2

Planning the Message

KEY POINTS

- ✎ A presentation is an extended conversation
- ✎ Use a theme to anchor your presentation
- ✎ Open with a bang, close with a zinger
- ✎ The middle can turn into a swamp

MESSAGE PLANNING

A presentation can be planned in an afternoon or over a period of several months—depending upon its complexity. Planning a major presentation usually takes several months. At the same time the message is being developed, the structure and format of the presentation will be evolving.

MESSAGE CONSIDERATIONS

Tone

There are many different ways to talk to people—you can be friendly, warm, excited and enthusiastic, breezy, demanding, commanding, rigid and uptight, ingratiating, or boring. Every conversation reflects your personality and mental state as well as the personality of the person you're talking to. It also reveals the pattern of interaction the two of you have developed.

Because a presentation is just an extended conversation, part of the initial planning is to determine its tone. Should it be formal or informal, uptight or relaxed? The purpose of the presentation, the personality and style of your presenters, and the level of complexity of the information you are presenting should help you decide. More than that, the tone should reflect the image of your company. What makes your company distinctive? How do you describe it to friends or other business associates? How can you make that personality come alive in a presentation?

We tend to say that business presentations must be businesslike. But what does "businesslike" mean? Does it mean serious, rigid, and boring? Does it mean warm and friendly? It's probably best to move beyond "businesslike" and try to define in more exact terms the image you want to project. How does your company's personality mesh with the personality of the client? Adjust your tone to reflect the situation. Remember it is a conversation, after all, and you don't want it to feel phony.

Three basic characteristics set the tone in most successful presentations: understanding, concern, and enthusiasm. Successful presenters demonstrate that they understand the nature of the problem, they are concerned about the client's future, and they are enthusiastic about the proposals they are recommending.

In general, most presentations use an upbeat tone that projects a sense of "relaxed seriousness." The tone is warm without being gushy, serious without being uptight and boring. The presenters are "loose"; they read the room and react to the responses that they sense. They know their message so well that they can phrase, or rephrase, the message for their audience. They aren't locked into an unchangeable script. Pitch the tone of the presentation to signal a team relationship. Let the client know that everybody is on the same team and working on the problem together. Use a phrase like, "Here's how we are going to get there" as it puts you immediately on the same terms and lets you transfer the ownership of the idea to them.

Timing

The tone of the presentation should also reflect the timing of the presentation. Gerald Schorin, a copywriter, marketing manager, and advertising professor suggests that attention is hard to control before 10:00 A.M. and after 3:00 P.M. Mondays and Fridays are both difficult days for presentations. He has found that attention spans are typically shorter in the warm, pleasant months and longer in winter. It's also difficult to keep anyone's attention right after lunch. If you can set the time, choose 10:00 on a midweek morning. Sometimes the time is unilaterally set by the client and you can't do anything about it. Tony Wainwright tells a story about competing some years ago for the Iran Airlines account. The client chose July 4th, which is not only a holiday, but fell on a weekend that year. "It was our holiday,

A presentation is just an extended conversation

If you can set the time, choose 10:00 A.M.

not Iran's.'' The time of the year was another factor. ''It was a hot, muggy day in New York when the Generals filed in to our office.'' But Wainwright wanted the business and did what had to be done. Sometimes a potential client will test you this way just to see how accommodating you will be—how badly you want their business.

If you are presenting at difficult times, Schorin suggests using a format that allows for shorter, punchier delivery. He also suggests:

- Using an outline handout and other techniques to make fewer demands on the audience

- Keeping the material simple and reducing its complexity

- Using variety, alternate speaking styles, move from slides to boards

- Saving long, involved expostulations for the plansbook

Order

The best times, in terms of the order of competition, are first or last; the worst time is in the middle. Tom Hagan explains, ''Last is probably best if you understand that everyone else has superseded your 'ordinary' ideas. But being last gives you the last shot at the prospect. If you're first,'' he says, ''you can still 'supersede' the competition by putting down all the 'ordinary' ideas the prospect can expect to see in the subsequent presentations. Then anyone who does present an idea you've already rejected becomes discredited.''

Hagan says he has seen presenters working in a difficult time period use extreme measures to wake people up. ''I've known presenters who had to go on after lunch who have had the entire room stand up, shake it out, and go through some unique easy exercise that got everybody awake and alert and sympathetic.'' Many kinds of activities can be used to beat those afternoon blahs. Ask the audience to get up and look at materials presented in poster format and mounted on the walls. Take a break in the middle so they can get coffee. Ask them to help you change the furniture around or move their own chairs. These are some of the less obvious ways to get the adrenaline pumping.

The secret in coping with the time slot is to plan around it. Hagan says, ''Wherever you end up in the sequence, give it some hard thought. If you don't like your spot, try to maneuver to change it. All is fair. If you can't change it, try to come up with a creative gimmick that neutralizes your bad position, or turns it into an advantage.'' But don't lose sight of your main objective: presenting and selling your ideas. Don't get so concerned about a bad time slot that you blow what you have to say.

ORGANIZING THE MESSAGE

In many cases, your presentation will have a highly complex message based upon voluminous facts and research data, a sophisticated and intricate strategy, and carefully developed conclusions and justifications. The challenge in developing a presentation is to condense all of your material into a message that is absorbing and easy to listen to.

Theme

If you want your presentation to be memorable—and that's important in a competitive situation—you may want to anchor it with a strong theme. Give the presentation a title that establishes the theme. Develop a symbolic visual. Tie it all into the client's business or problem. Concepts like playing cards, games, building blocks, recipes, pathways, highways, and street signs have all been used as thematic anchors for presentations. The theme should be relevant to your plan. If you are presenting the Marlboro campaign, for example, then use a Western theme; if you're presenting a sweepstakes promotion, a casino theme might fit. Don't get too cute, however. The theme should never override the message.

———— **Use a thematic anchor** ————

Ogilvy & Mather used a picturesque postcard theme to help land the Illinois Tourism account. The agency's idea was to make state residents aware of the many local attractions. To sell it to the tourism board, Ogilvy & Mather printed dozens of cards featuring scenic spots in Illinois using the tagline, ''This weekend you could be here.'' The agency CEO mailed them out with personal notes to members of the tourism board staff. At the presentation, they opened by saying, ''We're the postcard people.''

When BBDO went after the Apple account, Phil Dusenberry gave the presentation. ''In contrast to competitor and long-time Apple agency Chiat/Day, he breezed through the marketing part of the campaign and then focused very quickly on the theme and the creative. After extolling the merits of ''magic words,'' he presented the theme line: ''The power to be your best.'' Then he explained the power of the theme, showing how it could work equally well with the home, education, and business markets. John Sculley, then CEO of Apple, hearing exactly the kind of theme he wanted, gave BBDO the account over long-time agency Chiat/Day.

Key Points

From the enormous amount of material collected during research and planning, you must sort out the best facts and ideas. What key points do you want your audience to remember? These key points are the critical pieces of information on which the logic of your proposal will be built.

Keep in mind that your audience's retention is limited. Highlight a few ideas in each section and do everything you can in the presentation to make them stand out. One strong key point well planted in memory is better than a poorly remembered laundry list.

Writing key points is like writing an ad. You telegraph your idea through memorable phrases like those in headlines, subheads, and taglines. Then you anchor your message in the audience's memory by repeating these key phrases.

To identify key points, get together everyone who is involved in developing the plan. Put aside everything—all the research reports, the strategy statements and copy platforms, the memos—and just talk through your proposal. What comes to the surface in this free-wheeling run-through are the key points. Make sure that they will be key points in the client's eyes, not just yours. Check by bouncing them off your client contact sometime before the presentation.

Openings

The opening and closing are the two most important parts of the presentation. You might consider writing out and memorizing these two sections. They are the places where you are most likely to reveal your inexperience.

The function of the opening is to seize attention immediately and establish your credibility. Remember, the audience is judging you. They will probably start off liking you unless you make a bad impression in the beginning. Untrained speakers often start with either an apology (''Sorry we're late,'' ''The visuals aren't finished,'' ''I've never done this before and I'm really nervous'') or with an unfunny story. All of these can blow your natural advantage. Many speakers also suggest avoiding phrases like ''How are you?'' and ''How's it going?'' Sales writer and speaker Kerry Johnson says, ''These are greetings that are particularly thoughtless in generating rapport. When was the last time someone told you how he felt just because you asked him how he was?''

> Your point of entrance should be a point of concern to the client

Humor is very difficult to handle in a presentation. For centuries, toastmaster groups have been telling speakers to start with a joke. Unfortunately, jokes are the hardest messages to communicate because they depend on timing and delivery. Inexperienced speakers rarely have the technique to make

---

EXHIBIT 2.1

INTERESTING OPENINGS

An opening, like a headline on an ad, should begin with something interesting. Some common techniques include:

- Deliberately arousing curiosity

- Telling a relevant or pointed story

- Bringing along a prop and holding it up while you make some comment about it

- Asking a question

- Quoting someone famous or someone important—particularly to your client

- Using a theme to tie your plan to your client's vital interests

- Citing some shocking facts

EXHIBIT 2.2

MEMORABLE CLOSINGS

Closing techniques include:

- Asking for the business

- Passing out a timetable, stating what needs to be done immediately if the timetable is to be met and asking to start

- Summarizing the most important key points

- Ending with a humorous touch to leave them feeling good.

- Summing it all up with a famous quotation

- Building up to some dramatic climax, some stirring idea

---

a joke funny, even when it is. Jokes are difficult to fit into a serious business presentation.

There are many ways to handle the opening, but your primary objective is to get attention and set the stage for the tone of the presentation. George Morrisey, in his book on business presentations, gives a number of suggestions. You can start with some direct, but dramatic, statement involving the client's business—perhaps a fact you've uncovered from research or a significant quote from a key player. You may tell a story or set up a vivid example. The thing to remember is that whatever technique you use, you should focus on something that matters to the client or prospect—not just tell some interesting or cute story. The point of entrance should be a point of real concern.

Closings

A lot of presentations don't end; they just wind down. There is nothing more to say so the presenters stop talking and sit. That is not an effective use of a very critical part of your presentation.

The conclusion should anchor your recommendations firmly in your client or prospect's mind. Like the ending of an advertisement or commercial, it is where you structure in everything you can to intensify memorability. Presentations have to be planned the same way. What is it that they must remember a week later? Is it a key strategy recommendation or a dynamite slogan? Where does the brilliance lie in your plan? Hit them with that again at the end. Here are some suggestions:

- Use handouts

- Prepare a large, arresting visual

- Pause dramatically and then slowly repeat the point again

- Do something dramatic; close with a skit
- Hold up a large banner

Don't let your presentation run down, break down, or run on and on. You should quit while your audience is still interested, not after they have stopped listening. What they hear last is what they remember longest, so leave them with your final words ringing in their ears. Make your conclusion a real zinger.

In addition to reinforcing the memorable element, closings also give direction to further action. What should the client do next if they agree with your recommendations?

PRESENTATION OUTLINES

Some universal outlines that work for most presentations are based upon standard speech techniques yet take into consideration the need for both informational and persuasive material.

Basic Sections

One presentation outline used by the Burson-Marsteller Agency identifies four basic sections:

1. The opening: establishes tone, gets attention
2. The statement of position: sets the goals and objectives, identifies the problem and proposes a solution
3. Supporting evidence: provides relevant data and research findings, logically developed justifications
4. The closing: summarizes and restates the benefits to the listener

Business Outline

A more elaborate outline has standard sections that typically are found in most business presentations:

1. Opening: focuses attention on the charge or mission of the plan
2. Situation analysis: key areas and the important points about each area
3. Opportunity recognition: analyzes the needs and identifies the problems
4. Recommendations: presents the solutions to the problems just identified
5. Rationale: provides the logic and justification needed to support the recommendations

6. Defense: anticipates the objections and answers the expected questions

7. Summary: repeats the key points and highlights the logic

8. Call to action: the closing identifies the next steps and asks for decisions

These are the common sections, or steps, used to develop an argument or position. This business outline is based on the approach recommended by rhetoric teachers since the time of the Greeks: tell them what you are going to tell them, tell them, and then tell them what you told them.

The actual order can vary. Some presentations start with the key points and then use the rest of the presentation to explain and justify them. A more dramatic approach starts with the problem and builds up to a climax as various pieces of the solution are disclosed. The first approach is more rightbrained; the second is more leftbrained. You should match the approach to your agency's presentation style.

Campaign Plan Outline

Another kind of outline is imposed by the content of the message. When you are presenting a complex document like an advertising campaign plan, the presentation should reflect or follow its organization. Most advertising campaigns include the following functional sections:

1. Situation analysis: contains the research findings

2. Strategy: outlines the key strategy decisions such as target audience and objectives

3. Creative: presents the creative strategy and executions

4. Promotion: if needed, this section includes sales promotion and public relations proposals

5. Media: presents the media strategy and details of the media buy

6. Evaluation: presents proposals for evaluating the success of the campaign

7. Budget: this section wraps up the costs for all aspects of the campaign

Organizational Strategy

Organizing a presentation can be extremely complicated since you are structuring both the logic of the argument and the functional sections of the plan. There are a number of ways to organize a campaign presentation, for example, and what works in one situation may not work in others.

Some planners believe strongly in a straight-forward businesslike approach. They would have you introduce your plan, develop and substantiate your recommendations, and close by restating the key points. In effect you are introducing all of the recommendations at the beginning, then developing them during the rest of the presentation. Executive summaries are useful with this approach.

Another technique is to build one point at a time. This is like the conventional plansbook outline where you go through the plan section by section, explaining each topic as a discrete unit.

Others like to disclose the brilliance of the logic little by little, building up to a dramatic climax. This approach uses a variety of techniques to involve the audience in the construction of the logic. For example, you may ask leading questions whose answers set up the next recommendation. You may use your visuals to "build a wall," using each visual to disclose a key element of the plan.

Gerald Schorin recommends building up to a climax. He suggests putting the strongest sections near the end. Furthermore, he says, "nothing ruins a climactic presentation as much as following the gangbuster creative with interminable details of media or research methodology."

The budget is a good example of a section that can be handled several ways. You can start out by stating the budget since, to a certain extent, that determines the scope of the effort and is necessary for perspective. You can also build the budget and close with it at the end after you have discussed all the budget items. Or you might do both—state the level in the beginning and come back at the end with a detailed wrap-up of the costs. If it is the client's budget, it is okay to start with it. However, if your proposed budget might be a surprise to them, presell it and build up to it. Clients are very budget-conscious and the whole plan may be thrown out if the budget presentation is mishandled.

While Gerald Schorin is right that numeric information like budget figures may dull the climax, it is still considered good salesmanship to save the costs until the end. If you disclose the costs too early, you may chill enthusiasm. John Grant makes another recommendation. He has had good luck suggesting a follow-up meeting to talk about and work out the details. This is a useful technique for handling media numbers as well.

BUILDING AN ARGUMENT

Every plan is compiled from a set of recommendations. Each recommendation is based on an analysis of the problem that includes an idea for its solution. Most presentations are built on proposals that need justifying. The clarity of the logic that justifies these proposals determines how persuasive the presentation will be.

LOGIC

Structure your message in short digestible segments that pivot around the key points. Logic is the internal connection between the key points, the reasoning that ties one point to another and leads to a conclusion. It helps the audience follow the argument from point to point.

Your presentation has to state your proposal clearly and build a strong argument by directing attention to the important points. A big problem with many presentations is that they communicate too much information much too quickly. Then the message is muddled and the logic is not clear.

The Logical Approach

The organization of the presentation demonstrates your ability to approach problem solving in a logical manner. If your presentation is well organized and easy to follow, then you've demonstrated your skill and built your credibility. As Dale Carnegie says in his book on public speaking, a presentation is "a voyage with a purpose and it must be charted." Organization, usually done by outlining and scripting, is how the voyage is charted. According to Carnegie, "The person who starts nowhere, generally gets there."

> How you organize your presentation demonstrates how you solve problems

Weaving Together the Logic

When you move to the body of your recommendations, you are constructing a web of logic built on supporting documentation. Several techniques can be used to support the logic of an argument. Benchmarks are used in before-and-after studies and in projections. They help establish how high is high. A benchmark can be derived by analyzing a parallel situation. Benchmarks and parallel situations are often used in advertising to justify and explain objectives. Analogies and metaphors are techniques of comparison. They can be used to make a point or illustrate a process. Another type of support for an argument is expert testimony.

A presentation technique that helps illustrate the connections between points involves "building a wall" with all of your key points. If there is a bulletin board on the wall, use it with masking tape or push pins. A free-standing, hinged bulletin board can also be used. After you are finished with the presentation, the logic is clearly displayed for everyone to follow. Use "the wall" to summarize the key points of your presentation.

A playlet with a little drama and suspense could illustrate the situation in which the company finds itself. Dramatic techniques have been used to good effect by agency presenters. Play a game of "what if . . . ?" What if brand awareness were 60% rather than 25%? What if trial was 40% rather than 10%?

You might also introduce one set of conditions, then bring resulting events full circle to show the impact of a different set of conditions. Or you could start by sketching the dilemma your client is in. Change the conditions with your plan, and watch the hopelessness change to hopefulness. "What if" is a technique for circumventing the occasional prohibition against presenting creative in a new business presentation. Even in a regular client presentation, "what if" can often substitute for expensive creative executions.

Logic and Support

The logic of the selling premise should be more than just a string of cheerful, but empty phrases. Sales people call this "pumping sunshine." Most executives have little patience with unsupported promises. They want solid justification and documentation. Don't try to snow them. Be enthusiastic, but don't be ridiculously positive.

DOUBLE-SIDED ARGUMENTS

If you present the facts and arguments on both sides, and then let the conclusion follow what you hope is the obvious logic, you involve your audience in building the recommendation. The conclusion is much stronger if the clients arrive there themselves.

You don't want to shoot yourself in the foot, but a statement that acknowledges limitations and potholes has a lot of credibility. If there is an adverse point, include it in your presentation rather than waiting for the client to find it. By promising too much, you can oversell yourself right out the door. But if you realistically and honestly appraise your proposal's chances of success, your presentation will be much more believable and impressive. The British have long known that there is persuasive power in understatement.

Disarm them—give both sides

SHARPSHOOTING

Another strategy to consider is trying to out-maneuver your competition. There are many alternative ways to solve any problem. Likewise, all data can be interpreted in a variety of ways. If you are competing for an account, then you may have determined what the obvious or common approach to this problem might be. Use the argument supporting your position to knock holes in a position you think someone else might take. Tom Hagan says that "with a little humor you can belittle the ordinary, the obvious. Then when someone else comes in with that idea, the client will likely snicker." Hagan describes a presentation his agency made to the Colorado Lottery. "Our first idea was to use the very distinctive Colorado license plate. Then we figured everyone else would use that same idea so in the presentation we had a mock up of an ad using the license plate which I tossed to the side while giving eight reasons why that idea wasn't good." Sure enough, the competition all came in with the license plate idea.

Another strategy is to get there first or make your presentation bigger and better. Tony Wainwright describes an opportunity the Bloom Agency had to be one of five contenders for the regional Wendy's business. "We knew that one of our competitors would 'put on a show,' " he says, but the

Bloom crew decided to outdo them. "We wrote some original music, had some of our young ladies dress up in Broadway costumes and did an opening night extravaganza." How did it go? "Extremely well. We were on a high. Our client responded favorably. And we were awarded the account."

EMOTION

Persuasion isn't just logic, it appeals to both the head and the heart. Masters of advertising like Bill Bernbach have long known that you make the greatest impact when you touch people's emotions. "Reach out and touch someone" is more than just a glib advertising slogan.

Warmth

There is a place for emotion and feelings in most presentations. When we talk about setting a positive tone and building warmth, we're talking about the emotive effect of the presentation. When we say that the client needs to like you, we are talking about an emotional response. William Claggett, discussing new business pitches observed, "Most of us won't admit it, but the chemistry of the people in the room is often more important than the content of the presentation."

Acting Out

As one experienced presenter said about the magic of using some drama in presentations. "When you sing, dance and do funny voices you wake people up and focus attention. You make the material important." But acting doesn't just entertain and get attention—it can also rouse empathy and audience involvement. He explains, "If you do it with a smile and a lot of humility, you get sympathy." He suggests, "Imagine a bearded creative director imitating a Jewish mother or a toothless child while reading a proposed radio or TV script." Set up your audience. Tell them, "Here's where I do the little old lady bit . . . and if anybody laughs I'll kill you." Of course, they laugh, but, as he says, "It's appealing. People in the audience identify with the assumed embarrassment." You've touched them with your feelings. That's the magic hiding behind the logic of the message.

Trapping Attention with Emotion

Use emotion to focus attention and interest

Emotion can be used deliberately to focus attention and interest. Wainwright describes a presentation the Bloom Agency made to Pentax Cameras. "Our creative director brought her daughter into the meeting (in a tutu) and play-acted taking pictures of her little girl doing a ballet. Our audience loved it. And we got the account."

FOCUSING TECHNIQUES

Directing the audience's attention is a very important part of message planning. If their attention isn't under your control, it will wander. If their attention is wandering, they will probably miss something critical. Certainly they will have a harder time following the web of logic you are trying to weave.

Identify Critical Problems

One way to focus attention is to identify the critical problems to be solved early in the presentation. Ron Hoff, an expert on presentations, suggests that you start with a proclamation of purpose. Don't just "get underway." These proclamations are clarion calls; use them to focus attention and to anchor your analysis firmly in the clients' memory.

Develop strong phrases for the clarion calls. Like headlines, they should be attention getting, creative, and related to your client's business. They should strikingly summarize the key points of your strategy. These key phrases should ideally be "words with emotional significance" to your client.

Build on Points of Agreement

Another focusing technique, the affirmative premise, begins with a neutral point of reference which sets up a mental state of agreement. This is much stronger than a point which challenges the client's past operations and practices.

You want them nodding their heads in agreement from the very beginning of your presentation until you get to the point where you ask for the account or the decision. Paul Hirt describes this affirmative premise as "the head on the hinge." If they agree with your statement of problem they will be partners in finding the solution and, if they agree with your solution, then they have become co-authors in the plan.

Use Leading Questions

A related technique involves using leading questions in a logical progression to build up to your conclusions. Get them to agree with your answers to the questions, and then lead them right into your strategy.

Use Similarities

Another way to focus their attention is to develop a motivating dramatic idea based on some aspect of their business. This may be a case history. If you have solved a similar problem in the past, then use it to bring your point to life. Use case histories when situations are similar.

If you can base a metaphor for your plan on their operations, you will demonstrate your understanding of their business. For example, if they are in the express delivery business, a statement about care in delivering gold bullion could also express the idea that their business is a gold mine and your idea is a ingot of gold.

Dramatize

The situation analysis and the strategy decisions can be more than a dry summary of facts and findings. Dramatize your research. Bring in five pounds of computer printouts and slap them down on the table. Dress a team member like a delivery person for an express company and place a $5000 gold bar in front of the CEO. Playback some of the comments from your target audience that you heard in focus groups.

PROBLEMS

There are some techniques you might want to avoid in developing a persuasive argument. Don't arrive at conclusions without spelling out the supporting logic and facts. Avoid using out-of-date statistics and unknown research sources. Don't beg the question by throwing the problem back to the client.

Communicating the Unpleasant

Sometimes negative things that your client won't want to hear need to be said. Here are some suggestions to avoid having the client "shoot the messenger":

- Let someone else say it—use an audio or videotape from an interview or focus group

- Use an overhead or slide with comments from a questionnaire

- Repeat or quote their own people in their own words—use sales reps, distributors, dealers

MEMORY ANCHORS

In addition to designing a presentation that catches attention and flows logically from point to point, you also need to design for memorability. Most people only remember fragments of what they hear, and those fragments fade after several days. Clients who sit through three to five new business presentations will have a hard time remembering who said what. They may not be able to remember anything specific about your team's presentation unless prodded. In order to maximize the impact of your presentation you need to understand how your audience's retention processes work and how you can design message strategies that will intensify the memorability of your key points.

RETENTION CURVE

It would be nice if your audience came to the presentation all excited about your work and ready to concentrate 100% on your plan. Unfortunately, they may come to the meeting tired from a long day or a series of long days, emotionally wrung out from some traumatic experience in the office, or preoccupied with a problem they've been wrestling with endlessly. They may focus on your introduction, but their sustained attention is not a given—it's something you have to win and then maintain.

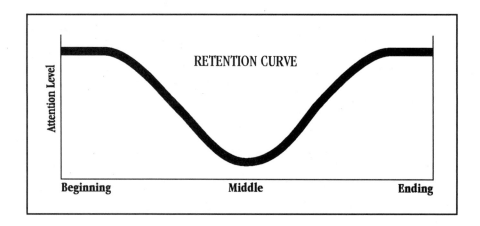

Beginnings and Endings

We know from the psychology of meetings that people are more attentive at the beginning of a presentation when they are still curious about what you have to say and at the end when they are looking forward to the conclusion. The middle is a swamp. You have to work twice as hard as their attention naturally starts to wander. Introduce all your key points in the beginning and summarize them at the end when people normally pay attention.

Middles

Do not introduce new points in the middle. The middle is for elaboration and discussion using dramatic techniques like these to keep attention:

• A deliberate change of pace

• Dynamic visuals

• Involving little playlets

- Leading questions

- Exaggerated statements for dramatic effect

Advertising uses these techniques to keep the attention of an indifferent or preoccupied audience. Remember, keeping attention through a presentation is much like keeping attention through an ad.

SCRIPTING

Structured yet spontaneous

The presentation message is developed through a process of scripting. It is rarely written out word for word, however, because a presentation that is written tends to become more of a speech and less of a conversation. It loses its spontaneity and the tone becomes formal and, in many cases, boring.

A presentation is structured, yet it projects a spontaneous or extemporaneous quality. It should maintain the feeling of a conversation where you are just "talking through" the proposal, but it should not lose sight of critical points and key pieces of logic. Furthermore, you have to "read the room" and adjust your message if you sense that it's not being understood or accepted. Scripting is a strange animal—structured, yet spontaneous and flexible.

PLANNING CARDS

To achieve both those qualities, the presentation is outlined using an abbreviated scripting technique. The planning is done section by section using "planning cards," or 3 × 5 cards with a key phrase on each card. (Examples can be found in the appendix.) Use phrases, not sentences. Try to capture just the essence of the message. Plan these key phrases like you do copy in an ad. They should be meaningful and memorable. While you want them to be catchy, avoid being too cute or flippant and don't use jargon. These cards carry three types of information:

- The key point

- Supporting key words, story ideas, explanation cues

- Appropriate visuals

These cards telegraph the key points and facts that provide the essentials of each recommendation and its support. By using cards you can edit and juggle the order without having to redo the entire section. They also serve as a guide to the visuals that will be used to support the verbal presentation. Your presentation will be given, not from a written script, but from a series of cards—eventually visuals—that state your key points succinctly.

SORTING OUT AN OUTLINE

Develop the outline by physically arranging these cards on a tabletop or pinning them to a bulletin board. A planning board, like a bulletin board, works best because the points can easily be arranged. Tabletops are easiest for preliminary outlining but take care not to mix up the cards.

Paul Hirt has a suggestion for outlining the body of the presentation, usually the hardest section to structure. Take all your 3 × 5 cards and shuffle the deck. Arrange them on the floor or table as a physical outline. Number them in order on the back. Then shuffle them again and again and place them in order over and over. Now see if these various attempts at arranging the cards result in a similar structure. Cards that show up consistently in the same place are logically arranged. Cards that are consistently in different places indicate logic that isn't clear. It could be an unclear key point, or perhaps you really do have several options for presenting that point and you simply need to decide which works best.

As you analyze your card outline, Hirt suggests you look deliberately for the threads of logic that lead from one section to another. More importantly, look for breaks or leaps in logic. Those are the places where you should recognize or insert a transition.

Also watch for branching. If too many branches lead away from the central topic, the logic may be hard to follow. Furthermore, watch where these branches go. Every section and subsection should contribute to your argument in some way. If a branch doesn't go anywhere, then it should probably be pruned.

You always have more information than you need, so you have to go through a continuous sorting process. To help evaluate your information, identify each point as a primary or secondary point. Analyze them in pairs and ask which point is more important. Continue to sort and eliminate until you are down to the absolute critical core of information. Remember no matter how hard the research effort was, or who contributed the information, nothing is sacred.

Politically speaking, however, if the research department worked for five days collecting data that you no longer are going to use, tell them why rather than letting them find out during the presentation. Remind them that the presentation only touches on the highlights, while the plansbook contains all the details. The research data may be a substantive part of the plansbook even though it does not appear extensively in the presentation.

Speak from key points on
visuals—not from notes

VISUAL NOTES

Your key points will become your visuals; your visuals, in turn, will be your notes for the actual presentation. As you practice you eventually will be able to speak from the visuals and move away from note cards altogether. The best representation appears to be done without any notes although the notes are on the visuals where everyone can see them!

EDITING

Editing is the single most important part of planning a presentation. You can't present everything you know or everything you have found out. Anything that isn't a recommendation or used in support of a recommendation has to go. Get to the good stuff. Most boring or confusing presentations are simply too long and throw too much information at the audience. It takes a skillful editor to make sense of it all.

How Much Is Enough?

How do you know how much is enough? Think about how you process information yourself. Give your audience enough information to put the key point in the right pigeon hole and connect it with other key points that are central to your argument. The points need to be coded and linked in order to make sense and be remembered.

According to Sharon Kalscheurer, vice president and a district manager for Axion Real Estate Management, most clients "are looking for a fairly brief presentation with specific answers to their questions. They just want to know the hard facts."

Clarity

Edit for simplicity and clarity. Your audience is made up of busy people who have many things on their minds. If your material is too complex, if the explanations are incomplete or missing, if the logic doesn't follow, you may lose them. Don't make big leaps in logic. Don't assume too much prior knowledge. You've been thinking about this proposal for a long

---

EXHIBIT 2.3

EDITING RED FLAGS

Most boring presentations can be saved by following these editing guidelines:

- Don't spend too much time building up or elaborating

- Edit out the dull, the predictable, the obvious

- Don't bother telling them something they already know

- Don't overwhelm them with too much information. Instead, create impact with key points that are highlighted and telegraphed.

time, but they are hearing it for the first time. Additionally, they may be hearing it after an argument, a missed deadline, or a rumor of some unexpected corporate disaster. Make it as easy to understand as you can, without being patronizing.

Four-Minute Frames

A good rule of thumb says that most sections should be boiled down to a four-minute frame. That is about how long your audience can focus on a section. Then you let up, make a transition, focus their attention again, and go for another four minutes.

Go back one more time and look at your key points and the logic that ties them together. Is the information properly prioritized? Are the key points obvious? Have you restated them? Endless repetition can be irritating to busy people, but the key points have to be repeated to establish their importance. One way to repeat without being obviously redundant is to use a ''build up'' visual or construct a ''wall.'' Finally, check again to see that the logic is clear and the conclusions are inescapable.

WELL-PLANNED PRESENTATIONS

Organization is critical if your message is to make sense and be memorable. Organization is also important in building logical arguments, and that's a critical part of persuasion. Scripting brings the whole process together and results in a carefully planned presentation.

CHAPTER 3

Selecting and Planning the Audiovisuals

KEY POINTS

✎ Use visuals throughout; seeing is believing

✎ Use visuals as signposts for your logic

✎ Visualize key phrases, relationships, comparisons, and numbers

✎ Slides are for showmanship; boards are for salesmanship

✎ Use audio to stimulate mood and imagination

In the previous chapter, we discussed planning and scripting the message. In this chapter we will focus on an equally important part of the message presentation—the audiovisuals. Because visual communication is particularly critical, we'll discuss how and when to use visuals, and how and when to use different types of AV media in presentations.

WORDS AND PICTURES

Like any other activity in business that costs time and money, a presentation is an investment. The way to double your return on this investment is to use visuals. People remember twice as much of what they see as what they hear.

Like a good attention-getting advertisement, a presentation message is communicated in two ways: through words and through visuals. The words express the concepts and the logic; the visuals elaborate, explain, reinforce, and dramatize the concepts.

VISUAL COMMUNICATION

Visuals are needed for direction as well as self-defense. If the audience doesn't look at what you are saying, they will look at the wallpaper, the burned-out bulb in the ceiling, or the haircut of the man in front of them. When you really want to concentrate on what you're listening to, don't you close your eyes? You've probably found that when your eyes are closed, your attention isn't diverted by things around you.

It's hard for people in our culture to concentrate on listening to a message for 30 minutes, particularly if that message is serious, involves abstract concepts, and is all words. This is why preachers have a tough time keeping their congregations awake.

We live in a visual age. Visuals are more easily understood and they communicate faster and more universally than do words. They have a riveting quality; it's hard to ignore anything that addresses our vision. Visuals are more attention getting than words, and they are more emotionally involving because they can be mesmerizing. Seeing helps us to understand, to believe. You know how much conviction is expressed in the comment, "I saw it with my own eyes." And from a presentation viewpoint, it's difficult to sell what you can't show.

We have become a visually oriented society. The average household television set is on almost seven hours a day. Television has had so much impact on the way we process information that it is difficult for us to understand something we only hear. Of all the information we receive, 85–90% of what we retain is presented orally and visually. According to a survey of 189 executives in 14 companies conducted by Raymond Slenski, president of Genesis Training Solutions, 89% said visuals are a "definite plus."

Thanks to *USA Today,* newspapers have become much more visual, using more graphics, charts, and colors to report the news. Stile Property, a property management firm, keeps a book of pictures and statistics from its various projects. When it pitches new business, it can use this file as drop-in material for presentations.

If you want to get and keep your audience's attention, use visuals. If you want them to understand the complexities of your message, use visuals. If you want them to remember what you said, reinforce your words with visuals.

> It's difficult to sell what you can't show

FUNCTIONS OF VISUALS

Visuals such as charts, graphs and illustrations add power to presentations. They create impact, stimulate interest, and aid retention. More than just a "visual aid," they carry the message as well as stimulate the attention and interest of the audience. They should be planned in tandem with the verbal and audio (words, music, or sound effects).

Memorability

Presentations using visuals benefit from the combined power of two channels—the ears and the eyes. Research has consistently shown that retention is higher when information is presented simultaneously in both channels. This is because the brain must do twice as much mental processing. The more mental interaction you can generate, the more thinking about your information the audience must do and the more impact and recall your message will have.

It is important, however, that the presentation be coordinated, that sight and sound work together. If you say one thing and show another, the messages will be at war with one another and neither will be memorable.

Memorability is a function of involvement which creates an indelible image in the mind. We file things in our memories by significant images that cue a package of related information. The image is like the tab on a file folder. We use it to code and then to sort and select what we want to retain. To enhance memorability, plan to use significant images. The Nestea plunge, for example, is attention getting but at the same time it demonstrates the refreshing benefit that is the main idea of the commercial.

Reinforce Logic

One of the important functions of visuals is to establish the logic, or outline, of the presentation. Some visuals will probably be in the presentation just to tell the audience where they are, like signposts. There are two types of outline visuals. The first is the sectional head or title slide. Like a chapter or sectional heading in a book, it separates major sections of the presentation and acts as a transitional cue both to the presenters and to the audience. The second type of outline visual is the subhead. Subheads are used to tell the audience where the message is headed. Both of these visuals simply show the major headings and subheadings from the outline prepared for the presentation.

Key Points

Visualize all key points

While the sectional heads and subheads are usually labels, another type of signpost functions like a headline and summarizes the key points. These are information statements. Rather than just saying "Sales," such a statement would say "Sales jump 33%." If you have developed a descriptive label for your target audience, for example, or if you are recommending a new slogan, then show it. It clarifies the phrase and anchors it in memory.

Most presentations include fundamental concepts such as market share, positioning, benefit strategy, budget allocation, and payout. These topics often serve as sections and should be identified visually with signposts. Their content, however, should be presented as information statements. For example, if current share is 24% and last year's was 20%, don't just visualize a big 24—show a plus of 4 percent. You want them to remember two things: that sales are up instead of down, and that they are up by 4 percent.

Clarity

One of the best ways to make sure your message is understood is to "show them" what you mean. Illustrate, dramatize and symbolize the key concepts. Show a picture of what you are talking about. Understanding happens when you say, "I *see* what you mean." If, for example, you have targeted a teen audience, show a picture of teens. If you are segmenting the teen audience, show a picture of the different types of teens you are referring to. Use illustrations or photographs—both will illustrate your concept and bring it to life. If you are talking about how important radio is to your target, show a picture of your target listening to radio. You can find visuals like this by cutting them out of magazines, newspapers, and ad clip books.

If you are discussing your targets' buying behaviors and their quandary in decision making, show a picture of your target trying to decide between two brands or products. Even still photography can dramatize something abstract like a buying decision. People remember images more than words. Leave them with an indelible image of that key concept firmly engraved on their minds.

Another type of illustration is the simple example. Show the obvious. When recommending a creative idea, show it.

Concepts like geography, schedules, calendars, weighting, segmenting, and growth patterns can't be easily explained. Talk about geographical strategies with a map, show schedules on calendars, discuss market share with a pie chart, show growth patterns with a bar or line chart, talk budgets with a simplified spreadsheet. These are all ways to visualize information that is hard to follow in words.

Numbers, in particular, are very hard to understand when presented in words. Show key figures, particularly big ones. Don't try to read numbers like $6,356,495.50; put them in a visual and round them off. When you're talking millions, the hundreds and thousands will never be remembered—let alone the odd cents. The previous number is a lot easier to read and understand when it reads $6.3 million. When you are comparing figures, use a chart to visually emphasize the comparison. The only way to understand clearly differences in size, scale, and frequency is by visually demonstrating the difference.

> Numbers need to be visualized to be understood

Identity and Image

Another important function of visuals is to make a graphic statement for your firm or team. Develop a presentation logo and a standardized visual format for all the visuals. The "cover" visual and all the "section" visuals should look alike. Design a "cover" visual that is uniquely yours and expresses the personality of your company or team. It should also work aesthetically. Package your first impression for maximum impact.

SELECTING AUDIOVISUAL MEDIA

Most professional presentations rely heavily on visuals to support and reinforce the message. Deciding what kind of visuals to use depends on how you plan the ''staging'' of the presentation.

In formal presentations and image presentations such as speculative bids to potential new clients, use slides or video. They give a slick show biz feeling. ''Showmanship'' is the key to this type of presentation. People are conditioned to believe that anything projected when the lights go down will be a whiz bang show. If it isn't, you may disappoint your audience. John Grant warns, ''Don't turn out the lights unless you have something 'magic' to show.'' Your audience's expectations may be higher than your slides are good.

Slides are not always appropriate. One presentation pro uses this rule of thumb regarding the use of slides and boards: use slides when the account is over $1 million and boards for accounts below $1 million. He admits that he really doesn't like slides because of their formality. Also the machine is noisy unless it's in a separate projection room. If you do use slides, also use a dissolve so the image change is not jerky.

Visuals can also be mounted on large posterboards and displayed on an easel, wall rail, or wall. In an emergency, they can even be placed on chairs. Boards are used for a more personal, conversational style of meeting. Individual presentation style is important when you are using boards because boards are less theatrical. The lights are up, eye contact is at a maximum, and there's more of a burden on the presenter to entertain. Most sales presentations are made using boards and ''salesmanship'' is the key.

A variation on the boards-and-easel style is to use a newsprint or layout pad with markers. This is a technique that lets you write as you go. As one agency executive explains, ''We use a lot of write-as-you-go messages and then cover a wall with them. We can go back to them and mark out or add things. It gives more animation, more excitement to the presentation.''

Overhead projection is used for practice presentations and in-house meetings. Some companies use overheads for campaign presentations and for research presentations because ''overheads make research findings seem more authentic.'' Overheads are usually restricted to in-house planning meetings because they aren't considered impressive enough to take to a major client presentation. Companies like A. C. Nielsen, however, often use overheads when reporting share and other market data to their clients. The big advantage of overhead projection is that you can speak with the lights on and face your audience, a reason for their popularity in education.

Video can be used for sections of presentations. Hagan says his agency uses video a lot. ''We use it for case histories when we want to point out similarities. Video is good; you don't have to turn down the lights, it moves, and you can add music.'' It has another hidden advantage. ''You can fool with the equipment; that gives you something to do for a change of pace.''

Boards are for personal chats

Hagan even uses video for radio commercials. "We put the lyrics on the screen and highlight them line for line. That way you can read the lyrics while you listen."

ADVANTAGES AND DISADVANTAGES

Two critical factors affect the selection of the appropriate audiovisual medium: the size of the group and the size of the room being used for the presentation. Slides, for example, work well for large groups and big rooms. Boards, on the other hand, work best in small group presentations. Video has a short viewing distance unless there is a large-screen viewer or multiple monitors around the room.

One big disadvantage of boards is that they are bulky. Generally they are hand lettered, and the professionalism can be affected by the quality of the lettering. They also have some built-in size limitations. The words usually can be seen best in a small to medium-sized conference room or classroom. Once you get more than 20 feet away, boards are hard to see.

If slides are well done, they can create dramatic visual effects. They can also be very expensive and relatively time-consuming to produce. If they are amateurish, they can be a real embarrassment. Slides can be projected to enormous images. They can be used in conference rooms and classrooms yet can also be projected to fill a screen in a large auditorium. If there is a chance that your presentation will be repeated for a large group, slides may be the best medium to use.

> Boards: small to medium size room
> Slides: any size room

PLANNING FOR THE MEDIUM

Early in the planning stage you should decide which form of medium to use. Your decision should be based on the presentation style of the individual presenters, the desired tone of the presentation, the room in which the presentation will be held, and the size of the group to be addressed. The amount of money and time available to spend on visuals is another factor you should keep in mind.

PLANNING THE VISUALS

Whether you decide to include slides, boards, or videotape in your presentation, you must invest time in planning their production.

PLANNING SLIDES

The most glamorous visuals used in professional presentations are projected from slides. They may be shot live, as in a picture of the target audience in a

EXHIBIT 3.1

HOW VISUALS COMPARE

	Advantages	Disadvantages
Slides	More professional than boards Suits all room and audience sizes Long life Visually versatile—color, pictures, imagery Dramatic—computer images can be dazzling Can carry in briefcase	Expensive: $25 to $75 each Long lead time—can take 2-10 days Needs electricity and viewing surface Lights down—presenter just a silhouette, audience may doze Restricts eye contact
Boards (professional lettering)	More personable Can revise quickly More professional than flip charts Moderate cost—$10 to $20 each Can be presented anywhere Moderate life Flexibility Notes can be written in margin	Can't be seen from more than 20 feet away Awkward to carry Takes 1-3 days to produce Limited to simple graphics Easily damaged
Flip Charts (self-lettered)	Least expensive Quickest: 1-2 hours preparation Easily correctable Shirt sleeve, working image Can be presented anywhere Can involve audience	Least formal Can't be seen over 20 feet away Requires lettering skill Awkward to carry Limited to simple graphics Pages get torn and dog-eared
Overheads	Can carry in briefcase Flexible Involving Inexpensive Easy to replace and correct Overlays can build up message Can look professional if typeset Can use with lights on Allows good eye contact	Projected image is seldom straight, can be distorted Distracting if placed upside down, slanted, etc. Speaker and projector can block screen Needs electricity and viewing surface
Video	Stand alone; saves time and money Interactive Good for groups of all sizes Can use with lights on Professional	Lose human contact Needs electricity and viewing surface Technical problems Corrections difficult Expensive and time-consuming to prepare
On-Screen Computer Presentations	Corrections and changes easy and fast Professional Wide color and graphic selection Can use with lights on Allows good eye contact With experience, presentations easier to design and complete	Requires expensive equipment Technical problems Needs electricity and viewing surface Awkward to carry

FIGURE 3.1

THE KEYSTONING EFFECT

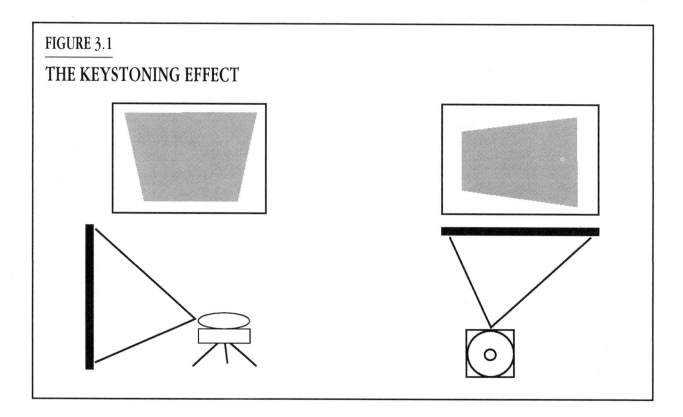

typical setting; they may be original art; or they may be art taken from clip-books or magazines that is shot using a copy stand. They may also be designed entirely on a computer and shot from the monitor or transferred digitally to film.

Shooting Live

To shoot people and scenes live, you will probably use a color slide film that can be easily and quickly processed. Most film processing labs can provide one day service on Kodak's Ektachrome. Other films take longer and you should check processing time with your film lab.

The film needs to match the lighting—use either daylight or tungsten film, or else compensate with filters. If you shoot indoors with daylight film, you will not have the correct color balance unless you use a conversion filter. For example, without magenta correction, daylight film under fluorescent lights will make an office scene appear green. Ted Vaughan, an AV expert, points out that "consistent color balance is an important attribute of a professional slide presentation."

You can shoot prepared art in a number of ways. The simplest way is to take it outside, mount it on an easel and shoot it using daylight film. You may have some problems with wind or bad weather. Another problem is "keystoning" which happens when the camera isn't perfectly parallel to the art and the image appears to be distorted. The projected image exaggerates the tilt and looks sloppy.

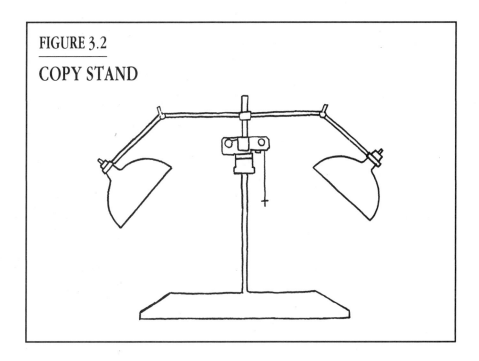

FIGURE 3.2

COPY STAND

Copy Stand Work

A more sophisticated approach is to shoot art indoors using a copy stand. With a copy stand, the camera is mounted above the art and the art is positioned flat on the base. Two light sources, either quartz or electronic flash, are positioned above the art and to each side of the camera. The lamps are usually at a 45° angle to the axis line between the camera and the art.

The most common lighting is 3200K photofloods. To shoot with this lighting, you need a tungsten color slide film such as Ektachrome Tungsten 160. According to Ted Vaughan, the preferred combination is strobe lights at 6500K and daylight film as it is "accurate and cool to work with—but it's very expensive." As a result, most copy work is done using Tungsten film and 3200K lamps.

An exposure meter, either hand-held or inside the camera, and a Kodak grey card are needed to figure the exposure, which will vary depending upon how far the camera is from the art and how much light the art absorbs. Use the light meter to check every shot. Using the grey card, you can establish correct exposure each time the distance from the artwork to the camera is changed.

Use a single lens reflex 35mm camera with adjustable shutter speeds mounted on a copy stand. Since regular lenses won't focus at less than three feet, you will probably want to use a macro lens. Be careful of exposure variations when using a macro lens to shoot extremely close distances.

A cable release will let you release the shutter without touching the camera and creating unnecessary motion. You also will need a sheet of non-glare glass to keep the art flat and reduce the reflection from the lamps on your copy stand. A polarizing filter can also cut down on glare.

A high-contrast graphic arts film (Kodalith or Ektagraphic HC slide film) can also be used for charts and slides. This gives a clear image on a black background. Panatomic X is also a possibility. If your film is processed commercially, it will be a special order that will take longer than overnight. If you have a darkroom available, you can process Kodalith yourself in a standard film can. You will need a different set of chemicals, though, so ask about them at your photo store. Color can be added to these high-contrast images by using sheets of colored acetate as a sandwich in the slide mount.

Polaroid recently developed an instant slide system that is useful in making presentation slides. To get instant slides shoot the slides using a copy stand; use Polaroid film and the Polaroid processor which is part of the system. You don't have to take the film anywhere to be processed and can see immediately what you shot.

Shooting Slides

Regardless of the method you use for copying your originals onto slides, remember to fill the frame when you shoot. Zoom the lens or move the camera until the image fills the viewfinder. Inexperienced slide makers often don't come in tight enough and the projected image has a sea of background surrounding a tiny image. When words are shot this way they may be too small to read when projected.

Production Houses

Unless you spend the majority of your time designing multiple-projector presentations, hire an expert. There are many tricks and intricacies to making these presentations work, and nothing is more embarrassing than having a big show get out of sync because its slides are out of order.

When you go outside to have a presentation done, talk to the production house early in the planning stage. They will show you just what can be done visually to enhance your message. A note of caution, however: don't get caught up in fancy gimmicks that are not only expensive but can detract from your presentation. Keep in mind that graphics should help interpret and emphasize a piece of information. When the visual technique is so dramatic and unusual that it calls attention to itself, it is counterproductive.

Optical Printers

Visuals are counterproductive if they are too unusual

Professional slide production houses use complex cameras called optical printers. They can make multiple exposures of graphics and words together, and add special effects and color. Optical printers are particularly useful for creating multi-image shows because they can expose several images on one slide. You can have a slide that appears to be split in half with two images side by side, or one that shows four images, each in a quadrant. As computer graphic slide systems are becoming more sophisticated, however, the optical printer is being used less often.

Computergraphics

Research shows that worldwide use of electronic presentation technology more than doubled between 1991 and 1993 and is projected to grow tenfold by the year 2000, particularly since software like Persuasion or Power Point is now available to design slides on a personal computer. Images—both words and pictures—can be created totally on computer. An image is digitized and the code then transferred to a slide processing system. With large computers and tremendous memory capabilities, these systems can create beautiful graphics with a tremendous array of color possibilities. The quality of the projected slide image is extremely professional. It is also now possible to use a personal computer to ''run'' a slide show presentation with the slides projected from the computer's software program.

If you create slides yourself on a personal computer you can either take the images to a film company that creates the slides on disk or transmit the image by modem. The quality of the PC-based systems is fast becoming as good as that produced by optical printers, and it's faster, cheaper, and you control the entire process. This field is developing rapidly, so you should do some research to find out about current systems and their advantages.

Multi-Image

The term multi-image is used to refer to different images seen on a screen, or screens, at the same time, and which may result from either the way the images are created or the way they are projected. Several images, for example, may be printed onto one slide, or they may be projected on a screen together using multiple projectors. Complicated multimedia shows can be created using any number of slide projectors, audio cassette players, or even film projectors and videotape players for a combination of still and moving images.

The simplest form of multi-image uses two slide projectors connected by a dissolve unit. The dissolve unit lets the images softly fade from one to another and automatically turns off the lamp in one projector while the other is projecting. On most dissolve units you can vary the rate of the dissolve from fast to slow. It is also possible to hold the dissolve units in the middle and create a superimposition. Some dissolve units can even record the slide advance instructions on an audio cassette tape so you can program your slides to an audio track.

If you are using two or three projectors, you may be able to coordinate the slides by hand, but it is very confusing. As you increase the number of projectors, you will probably want a computerized programmer that can record the slide advance commands electronically and then run the bank of projectors.

Scripting a multi-image show involves developing separate storyboards for each projector. These are usually set up vertically and side by side on a master storyboard format.

PLANNING PRESENTATION BOARDS

Boards need to be big and so do letters and illustrations. Most boards are designed on 22″ × 28″, 28″ × 44″, or 32″ × 40″ posterboard. They should be sturdy enough to sit on the easel without collapsing.

Lettering

Lettering on presentation boards is often done freehand by skilled letterers. Lettering takes a trained hand to look professional, so don't let someone talk you into using hand-lettered boards just because they like to print. The result can look like a junior high poster. Transfer type can be used but it gets to be expensive and transfer type has a nasty habit of getting nicked and then looking like they've been through a battle on their way to the presentation. Plastic letters are much better, though more expensive.

Mechanical lettering systems like LeRoy letters are fine if you have access to the equipment for them, most often found in school media centers. Stencil letters can look okay if you finish the connections between the letters, although you can leave the stencil look for effect. All these systems have an amateur feel to them.

Flip Charts

Flip charts are mounted with rings or spine binders at the top. Designed for use on a desktop, they are about the size of a large notebook.

A set of charts makes a free-standing book that the presenter can flip through as he or she talks. This is particularly good for one-on-one presentations. Typically they are printed in quantity and provided to a sales force for sales calls, although they can be individually prepared. When preparing desktop presentations for several people who will be presenting to different accounts, blank pages should be supplied so each presentation can be customized. While the natural home for flip charts is the desktop, they can also be designed in a large format for use on easels. There is a physical limitation to how big they can be and still be easy to flip. The easel shouldn't extend above the flip chart so pages can be easily flipped back.

Layout Pads

An interesting variation on a flipchart is a presentation in which you develop the visuals as you speak. In this case, the presenter works with a big fat marker and a large pad of layout paper on an easel. Key points are written on the pad as he or she talks. This is more informal in tone but it is tremendously involving.

The secret to pulling off a presentation like this is to write the words for each page in a light pencil in a corner. Only the presenter can see these cues. The presenter has to be able to print quickly and legibly while he or she is talking. It takes some practice. Even more impressive is the presenter with cartooning skill who can do art while talking. There is no danger of anyone's attention wandering during this kind of effective ''chalk talk.''

PLANNING OVERHEADS

The overhead projector is a wonderful tool for education and training sessions. It has moved into the conference room and is often used for internal business presentations. Overhead projectors are easy to use and, unlike slides, they can be used with the lights fully on. The overhead projector uses 8″ × 10″ clear acetate transparencies. Overhead transparencies can be prepared in advance using a simple office copy machine. Office-made transparencies are usually limited to a black image on a clear or colored background. With a thermafax machine you can get film that yields a clear image on a bright-colored background. Commercial copy centers can also prepare overheads in color.

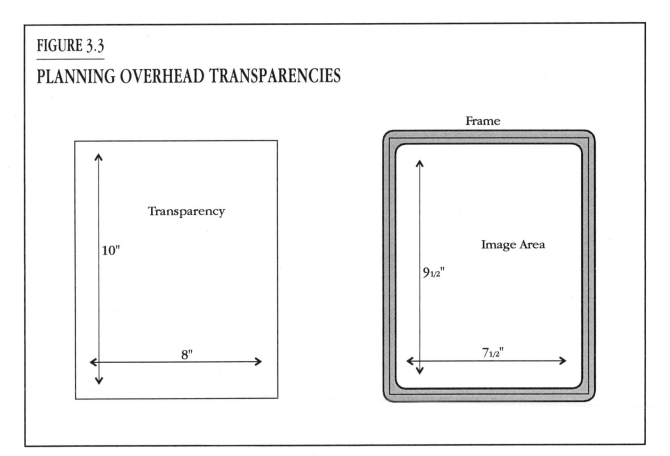

FIGURE 3.3

PLANNING OVERHEAD TRANSPARENCIES

Of course, you can prepare overheads by hand using a marker designed to write on acetate. Vis-A-Vis markers, for example, come in a variety of colors. You can also write or draw directly on clear sheets of acetate to develop the message as you deliver it.

Overheads are designed to be used in two primary ways: to make a recommendation or to report information. When used to recommend something like a new research technique or promotion plan, each overhead should be single-minded, carry only key points, have a logical flow, and follow the graphic rules for basic persuasive presentations.

The other use is for reporting periodic data like sales and share figures to a small group. To make performance data meaningful, it is generally necessary to show trends as well as numbers. In reporting quarterly sales data, for example, it is best to show the last eight quarters. This lets the audience look back over the history of the trend. Have sales been falling, or is this a new drop? Is the decrease greater or less than in the past for this particular item, quarter, or market?

When a page full of numbers is shown, the object is not for the audience to study all of them, but to be able to see the exceptions and trends such as significant changes in share, penetration, and purchase frequency. This type of overhead should be "pre-coded" using colored markers to highlight exceptions and trends.

At first glance, these all-number visuals seem to defy the rules of making presentations. Keep in mind, however, that your audience knows how to read figures. But even with knowledgable audiences, it's still a good idea to have summary charts that highlight major trends and findings. Above all, make sure the figures are large enough to be read.

PLANNING FOR VIDEOTAPE

Sometimes videotape is used in a presentation. Video clips can have great impact when they are used for verifying research results and showing creative concepts for ads or video news releases. For example, video can be used to record comments in focus groups and in support of key points. On video with thoughts expressed in their own words, research findings take on a very real and personal impact.

Before you decide to use videotape, think about the size of the audience and the room. A normal 19-inch screen can easily be viewed up to about a 20 foot distance. Beyond that you will need a second monitor or a large-screen video playback unit.

USING COMPUTERS

A computer can also be hooked up to large-screen projectors so that what is seen on the screen is visible to a large number of people. Some presenters like to show financial data this way to illustrate what happens when new data is plugged in. Working directly from computers allows presenters the opportunity to make last-minute changes in the presentation. However, many computer systems are not compatible with each other. All the necessary equipment to do large-screen projections may not be available at all presentation locations so check everything out in advance.

Pre-prepared charts and graphs are more controllable as you don't have to worry about computer glitches. Such visuals can be pretested to insure that they will be easy to understand; presenters don't have to fumble with plugging in numbers in front of an audience.

On the other hand, while Timothy Bryne, an account manager for Procter & Gamble, was delivering a presentation to a chain buyer, his numbers were challenged. Bryne was able to pull out his laptop and show statistics, planograms, bar graphs, and pie charts. "It's a lot easier and more convincing with the PC than having to poke through a briefcase full of computer printouts."

USING AUDIO

The audio in audiovisual communication is related closely to visual communication. Audio techniques are used in presentations to spur the imagination and create pictures in the mind. Slides may be shown to music that establishes mood or emotion. Taped excerpts from focus groups may be used to create a mental picture of the consumer that's better than anything you can draw in your mind from demographic data. Hearing their words makes these people come to life and adds impact to their comments. You may also want to use other kinds of verbatim excerpts, perhaps, from experts or other authorities, to bolster your argument.

Tony Wainwright describes a novel use of an audio medium—the telephone. During a presentation to Wendy's, "we sent one of our people into the field and had live phone conversations with him from a Wendy's store during the meeting."

Obviously, if you are presenting advertising, you may need audio to demonstrate your radio commercials. It may help to play the audio track while slides of the television storyboard are being projected.

In a presentation of creative concepts, cost and time make it unrealistic to produce finished original music for television and radio commercials. Several things can be done, however, to give the client an idea of what the final music will sound like. If it is a major creative assignment, ask the composer you hope to use to do a rough track. Even if it features only piano instead of full orchestra, the audience will get a feel for the tempo, style, and rhythm of the music. Or an excerpt from an already recorded piece can be used. For example, if you are recommending a 4th of July radio promotion and want to use patriotic music in the background, play a Sousa march.

Sometimes an agency has a staff member who can play piano or guitar and sing the lyrics. Obviously the quality of the performance has to be professional. Marion Dawson, long-time creative director and now partner in Dawson, Johns & Black, a Chicago agency, has on more than one occasion brought his guitar to a client creative presentation and strummed out the notes as he sang and read the copy being presented. His performances give the client an idea of the music being suggested, and add a fun bit of entertainment that keeps the meeting light and upbeat.

Music is available legally from commercial music libraries; sound effects libraries can provide all kinds of sound effects. Methods of payment vary with the library and the contract agreed upon. Like clip art, you can pay to buy the library and use any number of selections from it for no additional fee. If you want to use already published music, you will have to get permission and probably pay royalties to the composers and residuals to the performers. By composing and recording original music to use in your presentation, you can eliminate the problem of finding something you like or paying to reuse something already recorded.

Ted Vaughan, an instructional media professor, warns that you should ''strive for good recording quality. Poor sound will have a greater adverse impact on presentation effectiveness than will poor visuals.'' Every degree below perfect is a degree of distraction. If the tape is inaudible or scratchy, the audience will tune out. Also keep in mind that audio requires the proper equipment. Someone needs to make sure that the sound system is appropriate. If it is not a one-piece unit, care needs to be given to insure that the speakers match the amplifier. If that is not possible, the amp should be too big for the speakers rather than too small, according to Don Labiola, a contributor to *Presentations* magazine.

USING MULTIMEDIA

When presentations combine text, graphics, and sound into a synchronized package, the result is commonly referred to as multimedia. These are usually designed to run on sophisticated players as free-standing presentations. Although they can be impressive, designing them can take months of labor and thousands of dollars. With that kind of investment, companies tend to save multimedia presentations for presentations which need to be staged hundreds of times by a variety of people.

According to LaTresa Pearson, associate editor of *Presentations* magazine, ''Applications most suitable to CD-ROM (a common multimedia format) are those that require information to be distributed to multiple locations; mixed text, data, graphic and/or audio/video information; large data volumes; fast access time; and extensive searching, sorting and retrieval.''

Sophisticated digital techniques can sometimes be overkill, however. When MD Buyline Corp. of Austin, Texas, a provider of high-tech information for the medical industry, wanted to present a high-tech image it used a system involving a notebook PC, an 8mm video recorder, and a color LCD projector. According to Cecil Kraft, director of information services, ''We found that it detracted from the message we were trying to get across. The customer was awed by the technology. They often spent more time asking questions about the technology than our services.''

EFFECTIVE AV USE

The audiovisuals used in presentations may be just as important as the words used in the verbal presentation. The images are attention-getting and memorable, and they help lead the audience through the presentation. In presentation planning, you must carefully match the type of visuals to the setting, the client, the challenge of the assignment and the speaking styles of the presenters. Appropriate visuals will help you leave your audience with an indelible image in their minds. (See the Appendix for examples of AV formats.)

PRODUCING THE PRESENTATION

CHAPTER 4

Designing the Visuals

KEY POINTS

✎ Telegraph your points; design visuals like billboards

✎ One point per visual

✎ Use sequencing techniques

✎ Slides demand dynamite graphics

✎ Lettering; consider legibility and visibility

✎ Visualize numbers; use tables, charts, graphs, diagrams

DESIGNING THE ORIGINAL

The previous chapter discussed visual communication and the complexities of choosing media. This chapter will look at the design and production of visuals. In computergraphics, originals are created right on the monitor. All of the other techniques, however, require the creation of original art—illustrations, charts, words, or a combination of elements. This section will discuss design principles and techniques and guidelines for creating original art.

COMMUNICATION PRINCIPLES

Telegraph Your Points

In general, visuals should be simple and big. They have to be read at a distance, so they should be designed like billboards. Plan the visuals around

One point per visual

key words and phrases and use very few words—no more than ten. Don't put details and qualifiers on the visuals; your verbal explanation will elaborate. The words on the visual should trigger a thought rather than state a complete idea.

Design your visual as you would an ad. Use attractive, legible type with interesting, aesthetically pleasing graphics. Keep it simple and tightly focused. Be single-minded; only have one point per visual. Visuals should fit naturally into the discussion. They should contain information that is integral, not intrusive. Be sure to script the presentation so you are speaking about what the visual says. Likewise the visual should summarize the heart of the concept being discussed.

Sequencing

Remember your audience can read faster than you can speak. If you put up a list of items, they will inevitably leap ahead of you. And while they are reading ahead, they may very well be missing an important point. There are several ways to control this. You can put up a list and read the whole thing through, then go back and discuss it point by point. This satisfies the audience's curiosity. You can also use progressive disclosure where you uncover or add each point as you are ready to discuss it. These are called "build up" visuals. On slides, each new point is presented in a bright color while the already exposed points appear in a more subdued color. This focuses attention on the new point but allows the audience to refer back to those points already presented. To make them, shoot the base slide with the first point on it; then add the second point and shoot that slide; add the third point and shoot the third slide, and so forth. Then as you dissolve from one slide to the next, a new line will appear on the list.

On boards, flip charts, and transparencies, overlays help build up a message. The first point is on the base board; successive points are on clear acetate overlays. You can also uncover the points one by one. This is particularly useful with overhead transparencies, but can also be helpful with boards and flipcharts. On transparencies, place a piece of cardboard over the material and move the board down to uncover each item. On boards and charts, cut strips of paper the width of your board to cover each item individually. These can be easily removed in progressive order.

Format Consistency

The cover and sectional title pages should be designed together to create a consistent image for the presentation. Using the same design in the plansbook can visually tie it into your presentation, too. While a coordinated format is important, some visuals, such as those that communicate key points and illustrations, will require individual treatment. You can still maintain continuity by repeating the format design and graphic details or using color coding to indicate different sections or types of visuals.

EXHIBIT 4.1

ESTABLISHING FORMAT CONSISTENCY

Consistency of design involves a number of graphic decisions:

Using the same size format on the same background

Color matching and coding

Continuity in the use of identification elements like logos

Coordination in the use of type

Using parallel structure for phrasing

Consistent positioning of the type elements in the same place—should everything be centered, flush left, or indented?

Consistent punctuation and capitalization

Size is another important factor. Cut all your boards to a standard size and keep them all either horizontal or vertical. Mixing horizontal and vertical boards or slides will look sloppy, particularly if you are using slides and a dissolve unit. The most recommended approach is to standardize your slides in a horizontal format. It may be hard to make vertical pages fit a horizontal format, but it's better to have the extra margin than an inconsistent format. It is just as difficult to show television frames in a vertical format. The solution is to stick to horizontal. We are used to seeing projected visuals in a horizontal frame.

Boards can be any size, but slides have to be done to a 3:2 ratio. In the appendix there are sample frames for designing slides as well as frames to use in scripting the presentation.

Boards and slides usually are given a standard treatment for type, rules and borders, color, and little identity details like logos. If you are doing slides, you might make a master format on clear acetate with all the borders in place. Place the acetate over the type when you shoot each slide, and then you won't have to do the borders again and again. You may want to do a lettering master if you are using transfer type. Position the guide under the paper on which you will set the type and use it for aligning the letters. This works well on a light table. Using the same size paper for your slide originals (9″ × 6″ works well) can also simplify and standardize production.

Watch what you paste in place on your slide originals. If you cut out art and paste it down, the camera may see the cutouts and the shadow lines. If you use a Kroytype system for typesetting, for example, your letters will come out on a strip of clear acetate. You can position them on the visual, but the camera will see those strips of acetate and also any guidelines you may have drawn to help with the alignment. The solution is to make a photostat

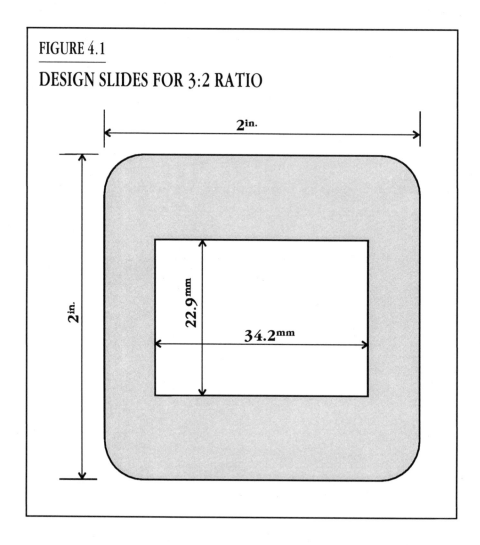

FIGURE 4.1

DESIGN SLIDES FOR 3:2 RATIO

or photocopy of your original and shoot from it. The photocopier isn't anywhere near as sensitive as a camera, so it won't pick up the shadow lines. Color can be added to the original art by using a marker or colored transparent acetate sheets.

Use Dynamic Graphics

Slides demand
dynamite graphics

Slides are an entertainment medium so the graphics need to be dynamite. Art for slides and boards can be handdrawn, clip art, cut out from some other medium, or copied from books. Be careful about copyright violation, however. You can even use still photographs. Previously published illustrations can be photographed on a copystand.

To add letters to the illustration, position transfer type on clear acetate over the illustration. White transfer type will create reverse lettering. A dramatic photo from the company's annual report, for example, can be used as a sectional slide with the name of the section superimposed in either black or white letters.

PRODUCTION CONSIDERATIONS

TYPOGRAPHY

Letters on visuals can be produced in a number of different ways. Handlettering, mechanical lettering systems, and transfer type are used on boards. Typesetting and transfer type are commonly used for slides. Mechanics are critical. Sloppy or uneven lettering, a problem on handlettered boards, can be a real distraction on slides because the relatively small original is projected to many times its original size.

Typeset letters give the most perfect typographic image and, with the advances in computerized typesetting, typeset quality is becoming easier to achieve in-house. A personal computer with a laser printer can create acceptable type for slides and tabletop flip charts. If you use a stat camera to enlarge type you can create typeset visuals for boards. Sans serif type, being a bolder letter form, is recommended over more delicate serif lettering.

Letterspacing

Another detail to consider carefully is letterspacing. Letters typically are typeset quite close together. Amateur lettering often allows more space than we are used to seeing between letters. It's also critical to adjust the space around the letter to compensate for letter shape. Letters that are tall and skinny, like *I, 1,* and *t,* need more space around them. Letters that are fat and round, like *o, c, m,* and *w,* sit closer together. Letterspacing compensates for the visual weight of the letter.

Legibility

Once again, the most legible visuals are big and bold. According to David Peoples, former IBM consulting instructor, ''A good visual aid should look like a billboard on an interstate highway that people are going to read while going by at 65 mph.''

Contrast is an important factor, too. If you are using color for either the type or the background, plan the color combination to create maximum contrast. Black creates the greatest contrast with either yellow or white. Black, however, does not contrast well with blue, green, purple, or brown. Likewise, color combinations like light blue on beige or white on yellow have very little contrast.

With visuals in print and on boards, dark letters on a light background are considered easiest to read. Reverse lettering, which gives the appearance of white letters on a dark background, is harder to read because we are accustomed to perceiving the dark areas as foreground.

The opposite is true with projected visuals such as slides. The black you see in slides really represents the absence of light. Since our eyes are attracted to light, we focus on those areas where light is projected and the image is

FIGURE 4.2

TRANSFER TYPE

bright. If the background is all projected white light with dark letters, the slide is almost blinding. Therefore, most word slides are designed with the letters reversed out of a dark or colored background. If you use yellow letters on a black background, the background on the slide simply disappears because it is only a blank area where light is absent. The letters, in contrast, are seen as yellow light and are very attention getting. It's a good idea to avoid bright colors for backgrounds or secondary elements.

Some color combinations are particularly tiring to the eyes when projected. When used together, bright reds and bright blues or greens assault the viewer's attention because both are fighting for attention at the same time. This creates eyestrain. The colors may even seem to vibrate.

Most of the research on legibility comes from the billboard industry, which is dedicated to finding what works best for reading at a distance. Besides recommending maximum contrast, they recommend using bold rather than delicate letters and simple rather than complex designs.

VISIBILITY

The biggest problem with visibility is size—and not just the size of the board or screen. The size of the letters is critical, and that depends on the viewing distance of the audience relative to the size of the screen or board.

Viewing Distances

Kodak has studied viewing distances and has developed a formula to help determine the appropriate size for the letters. Assuming you have a screen of adequate size for the room you're using, Kodak recommends that the minimum size for the letters should be $1/25$th the height of the screen. For example, if you are using a screen that is 5 feet tall, the minimum letter size should be approximately 60 inches divided by 25, or $2^{1}/_{2}$ inches when projected. If you are using a posterboard that is 24 inches high, your minimum letter height would be approximately 1 inch, or 60 point type. (In type sizing, one inch equals 72 points.)

Size of Letters

For slides, what you really want to know is not the size of the screen image, but the size of the original you are creating. To be visible, how big should the letters be on the original art? The easiest way is to set up a format based on the proportion of a slide image which is roughly 3:2. If your originals are being created on cards that are 10 inches wide and 8 inches high, the projected image will be proportional to the original you are designing. You can use the same $1/25$th rule to identify the minimum size of the type on your original. For example, $1/25$th of the 8 inches is roughly equivalent to 24 point type. Thus the minimum type size for originals created in 10″ × 8″ format would be 24 points.

And that's only the *minimum*. Use bigger letters for more impact. Text is often set in 32 or 48 point for slides. If the slide text is 24 or 32 point, consider using 60 or 72 point type for headings.

EXHIBIT 4.2

MINIMUM TYPE SIZES FOR ORIGINAL ART FOR SLIDES

Size of Original	Minimum Type Size
10″ × 8″	24 point
12″ × 10″	32 point

Screen Image

Another formula that considers the size of the room in relationship to the screen image can help you decide whether your calculated size is accurate. Kodak has developed an ''8H rule'' that tests how big the screen image should be for the room. The ''8H'' rule states that the maximum viewing distance is equal to 8 times the height of the screen, assuming you fill the screen with your projected image. For example, if you are using a 4 × 4 foot screen, then the 4-foot height times 8 equals a maximum viewing distance of 32 feet. So a 9″ × 6″ original with 18 point type can be projected safely to an audience as far away as 32 feet on a 4-foot screen.

EXHIBIT 4.3
SCREEN AND ROOM SIZE

Screen Size	Projection Distance
3 feet	24 feet
4 feet	32 feet
5 feet	40 feet

The same principle holds for boards and flipcharts except you work backwards to determine their size. If your farthest viewer will be 16 feet away, your board height will need to be at least 16 feet divided by 8 (2 feet, or 24 inches). To figure out the *minimum* letter size, calculate $1/25$th of 24 inches. The result is more or less one inch, roughly equivalent to 72 point type. To be safe, however, your letters can easily be two or three inches tall.

EXHIBIT 4.4
SIZES AND DISTANCES FOR BOARDS

Viewing Distance	Board Height	Letter Size (in inches)	Equivalent Point Size
12 feet	$1^{1}/_{2}$ feet	$^{3}/_{4}$ inches	60 points
16 feet	2 feet	1 inch	72 points
14 feet	3 feet	$1^{1}/_{2}$ inches	120 points

CREATIVE EXECUTIONS

A tough question to answer for most advertising presentations is how finished or ''tight'' to make the creative executions. It's a matter of investment versus communication. The closer the executions are to finished ads, the more accurately they will be seen and evaluated; but the more finished they are, the more they will cost to prepare.

PRESENTING PRINT

As with many aspects of a presentation, the level of finish depends on your audience and the type of presentation you are giving. If your agency is presenting annual campaign recommendations to a client it has worked with for several years, something between roughs and rough comprehensives will do. But if you are competing against other agencies in a new business pitch, full ''comps'' are needed.

One reason to stay away from tight comps is to avoid getting hung up on details. If anyone in the audience is nitpicky, you can end up discussing the color of the husband's shirt or the age of the oldest child shown in the executions. Roughs let you talk about the concept without focusing on the details.

Comps

Comprehensives, (''comps''), are recognized as the standard format for presenting promotional materials while they are still in the concept development stage. In standard comp style (see figure 4.3) the art is sketched in, all

FIGURE 4.3

SAMPLE COMPS

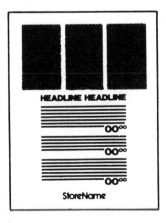

display type (headlines, subheads, slogans, taglines) is lettered in, and the body copy is ruled in. Sometimes the headlines are typeset. Photostatting comps will make them look more finished. Acetate overlays can give the ads a glossy appearance.

Copy

The actual copy for an ad or a brochure can be typed on a separate copy sheet and handed to the client after it has been read by the presenter. When layouts are mounted on boards, copy is often attached to the back as a backup. To present a print piece, set it on an easel or wall rail or tack it to the wall if the wall is made for presentations. Explain the visuals, starting with the headline and moving to the art. Then read the copy from a separate sheet of paper as the audience continues to read the piece. You usually won't see a print piece with final art and typeset copy. It is too finished. It suggests that you don't want client input. Furthermore, these materials always go through many changes before everyone agrees on the final wording. No sense setting the type while you are still in the discussion stage. A comp is the standard format for talking about an ad idea—stick to it.

PRESENTING BROADCAST

Audio

Radio can be difficult to present because it lacks a visual image. Unless you find some way to control their eyes, your audience's attention may wander. You can shoot slides of the typical listener's environment—in the home, in the car, looking at a billboard or stopsign—and use those slides to fill the "visual space." Or you can shoot the lyrics and have the audience follow along as they listen to the audio track.

Another way is to intersperse radio and television commercials and use the visuals from the TV commercial to reinforce the continuity between the two. One of the simplest visuals is a close-up of a radio being listened to by people in the target audience.

The audio is presented as a "demo tape." This is usually a piano or guitar rendition of the basic tune and rhythm. Sometimes one of the creative people who has some musical talent will sing or play a guitar to demonstrate the music being recommended.

Television

Television is hard to present because you have to use words to describe the plot of the story, the characters, the action, the audio, the setting, and the special effects. Television is presented with storyboards, a series of scenes sketched frame by frame. Each frame has room below it for the audio and video cues. You can make an oversized storyboard big enough for each individual in the room to see. If you are presenting in a large room, shoot the storyboard on slides, frame by frame, and project it as you play the audio track.

Some people have trouble understanding storyboards because they are so complex. A simpler alternative is to display one or two "key frames" as you talk through the story. This lets you direct your audience's attention without the distractions and confusions that develop with storyboards. If it's a soft drink beach scene, one frame may be enough. A product demonstration showing user satisfaction might require several frames. Use as many as it takes to communicate.

Slides and Video

Video can also be used to present storyboards. The frames can be filmed and shown while an audio track plays in the background. The same technique can be used with slides shot from the individual frames. If you are using an unusual technique or special effect, show a similar commercial to demonstrate the technique. Since some directors, like Joe Sedelmaier, can impose a distinctive style on a message, you might show something from the director's reel to explain this specific style.

VISUALIZING NUMBERS

Presentations are full of numbers—yet numbers are hard for most presenters to communicate, and harder still for the audience to understand. Presenters have to be particularly concerned about explaining numeric information when discussing media and research.

EXHIBIT 4.5

HANDLING NUMBERS

Numbers are hard to understand, and most people fear them. They see them as forbidding, overwhelming, intimidating. Keep these principles in mind when you present numbers.

1. People don't know how to listen to numbers, they must be seen to be understood.
2. If you have to give numbers verbally, keep them simple and round them off.
3. Give numbers one at a time if you are presenting them verbally. Give your audience space to assimilate the figure and translate it into a mental image.
4. Concentrate on what the numbers mean, what the relationships represent.
5. Use charts, graphs, and diagrams to visualize the relationships.

USING NUMBERS

Numbers are merely tools that measure and compare. In presentations, numbers are used to add credibility to recommendations and to prove conclusions. They are never as important as what they indicate. Instead of asking yourself what numbers you have to show, ask what findings you want to demonstrate to the audience.

Benchmarks

Raw numbers alone don't mean very much. To make sense of numbers, you have to work with them, symbolize them, show them in comparison, and visually demonstrate the differences in scale that they represent. Numbers usually measure something against something else. Express the scale clearly and provide benchmarks so everyone can see how high is high. For example, in some product categories you might be able to introduce a new product and immediately get a 17 percent share of market. The second year, you might project a 19 percent share for an increase of two share points, actually an 11 percent increase.

In highly competitive categories such as cigarettes or candy bars, you might feel great if a new product achieved a 3 percent market share. The second year you might consider an increase to 3.5 percent wonderful because you know that, however small it may seem in real numbers, it represents a 15 percent increase in share. A small percentage in actual numbers can sometimes represent a dramatic change.

Obviously, knowing how to handle numbers demands a basic competency in math. However, you also need to understand the communication problems those numbers represent. The first step in making sense of data is

---

EXHIBIT 4.6

VISUALIZING NUMERIC INFORMATION

There are a number of ways to package numbers to help your audience make sense of the relationships they communicate. Consider the following techniques:

—Tables

—Charts

—Graphs

—Diagrams

—Plots

—Schematics

—Pictograms

to isolate critical values. What is important out of all that data? Find the factors you need, and focus on them.

PICTURING NUMERIC INFORMATION

Charts and Graphs

The best way to handle numbers is to pull them out of the narrative and visualize their meaning. Instead of citing the numbers themselves, use charts to condense them and highlight their significance. Use the narrative to elaborate. Do not expect your audience to puzzle out the significance of the numbers by themselves. It is never as obvious to them as it is to you after you have gone over them several times.

> Charts condense and highlight numbers' significance

FIGURE 4.4

TABLE TURNED INTO A GRAPH

TABLE

Monthly Market Shares
(On a pound basis)

	Jan.-Feb.	Mar.-Apr.	May-Jun.	Jul.-Aug.	Sep.-Oct.	Nov.-Dec.
Brand Z	51%	54.4%	60.1	63%	67%	66.3%
Brand Y	49%	45.6%	39.9%	37%	33%	33.7%
	100%	100%	100%	100%	100%	100%

GRAPH

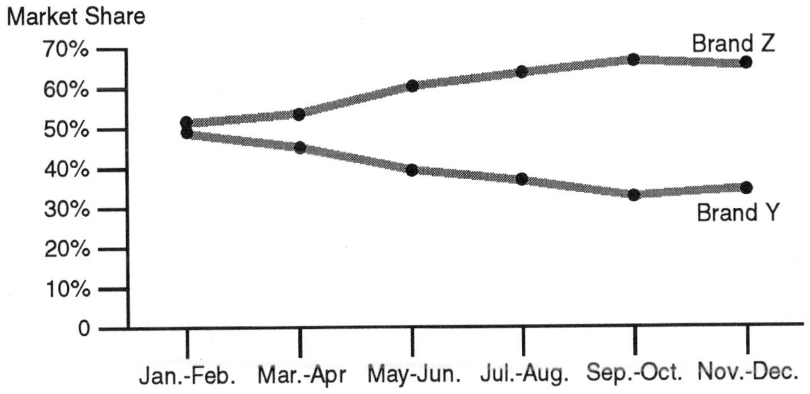

Numeric information is best expressed in charts, graphs, and diagrams. The word *chart* usually describes some kind of data arrayed in a graphic pattern. A *table* is a type of chart that is strictly numeric. It presents numbers, usually research findings. A *graph* depicts relationships and uses symbolism to represent the scaling of the relationships.

A set of numbers representing sales volumes, for example, is much easier to understand if it is expressed in a table instead of run-on text. A graph that uses horizontal and vertical dimensions to plot scale will be even easier to understand than the table. A three-dimensional graph makes relationships even clearer.

Every time you come across a set of numbers in your presentation, think about what the numbers are demonstrating and then think how best to symbolize this relationship. Just graphing a set of data may be enough to demonstrate your point.

Flow Charts

A flow chart is a good way to describe activities across a time sequence. Flow charts are used in planning to identify critical deadlines and the interrelatedness of relevant activities.

Flow charts are used in initial campaign planning to see that the plan is developed on time. Calendar flow charts are also used by planners to show the media schedule. A media flow chart summarizes media activities over a certain time period, generally a year or promotion drive period.

Flow charts can be used in presentations to describe the time frame and decision process; they can even be used to show how an idea goes from concept development and testing to execution. Other flow charts have other functions: a PERT chart (program evaluation and review technique) identifies who is responsible for what and when it needs to be done; a CPM chart (critical path method) identifies the most efficient way to get through a complex series of operations.

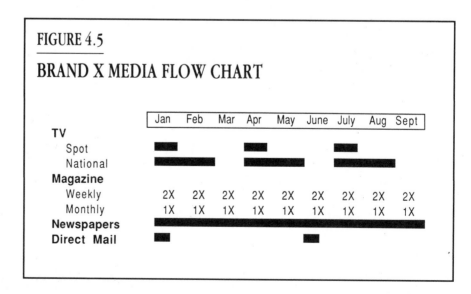

FIGURE 4.5

BRAND X MEDIA FLOW CHART

	Jan	Feb	Mar	Apr	May	June	July	Aug	Sept
TV									
Spot									
National									
Magazine									
Weekly	2X	2X	2X	2X	2X	2X	2X	2X	2X
Monthly	1X	1X	1X	1X	1X	1X	1X	1X	1X
Newspapers									
Direct Mail									

EXHIBIT 4.7

DESIGNING MEDIA FLOW CHARTS

Here are some helpful hints for making a media flow chart.

1. Thickness of the bars should proportionately represent GRPs and circulation.

2. In a plansbook, the number of gross rating points (GRPs) per week can be shown in each bar and the number of weeks under each bar. This is too much detail for a flow chart that will be projected in a presentation so omit it from such visuals.

3. Heavy-up markets and other spot schedules should be shown on a separate flow chart. Include all national activity since those markets will be getting this support along with the spot activity.

4. Don't list individual programs or periodicals on the master flow chart. If this information is particularly important to the presentation, make a separate chart.

5. For coupon drops via direct mail, magazine, or newspaper, show the drop week and then in a dotted extension of the bar showing the drop week show the time period in which 50%–75% of the coupons are expected to be redeemed. A coupon clearing house, like Nielsen, can provide this information.

6. Make sure the chart is fully identified, e.g., 1995 GREEN GIANT FROZEN CORN NATIONAL MEDIA SCHEDULE. Since flow charts are one of the most informative visuals in a campaign presentation, these slides are frequently removed and presented in a different context.

7. An agency presenting a media schedule to a client should make the bars on the flow chart as large as possible to fill the page. This will give the client the feeling they are getting a lot for their media dollars. Maximizing the weight of the media allocations will convince management it is getting a lot for its money. As long as everything is in proportion, it's all legal.

8. Develop the flow chart in a horizontal linear form with beginning activities on the left and the sequence of activities moving to the right.

Organizational Charts

An organizational chart is similar in format to a flow chart, except that it details job titles and responsibilities. It describes who oversees which activities and who reports to whom. Organization charts are usually developed in a vertical form with responsibilities flowing from the top down.

In new business pitches, organization charts are good to help show how management relates to one another and to the staff. They also outline the process of decision making.

Diagrammatic Charts

Also called schematics, diagrams are technical illustrations that visualize how something works. Diagrams are used to describe the parts or pieces of

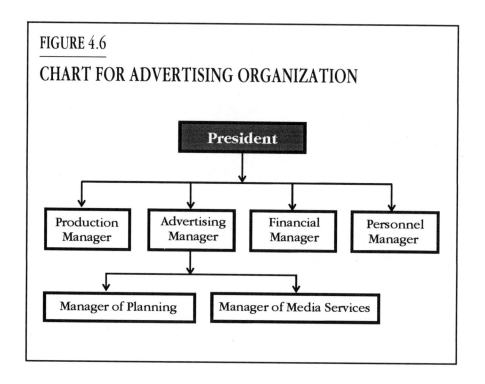

FIGURE 4.6

CHART FOR ADVERTISING ORGANIZATION

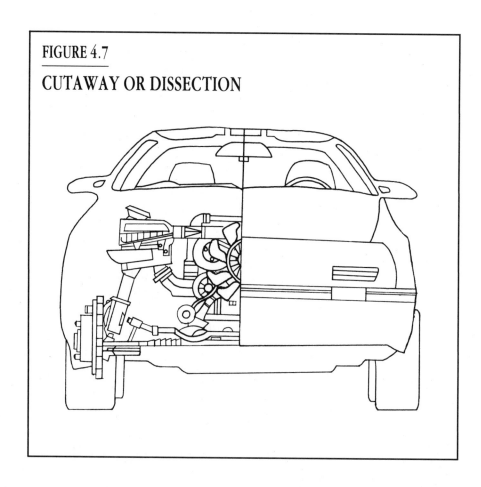

FIGURE 4.7

CUTAWAY OR DISSECTION

equipment as well as their position, location, and function. Cutaways are specific types of schematic diagrams that show the inside as well as the outside of something like a piston, candy bar, or clock. Cutaways are also called dissections.

Pie Charts

There are a number of types of standard graph formats and they all do different things. A pie chart, for example, is the standard form to use to depict pieces of a whole. Any time you talk about percentages, such as market share or budget allocations, that total 100 percent, a pie chart is a good way to express the relationships. As a rule of thumb, pie charts should not have more than six pieces. If a category's brand share is being shown, and there are 12 brands, combine all the smaller brands into ''others.'' If your brand is one of the smaller brands, it, of course, should be shown separately.

Start your largest section at 12 o'clock, with the other sections following in descending order. It is difficult to show how two sets of data compare using pie charts. Two pie charts side by side are really hard to understand. One way to deal with the problem of comparison is to use an overlay, although that may be equally confusing.

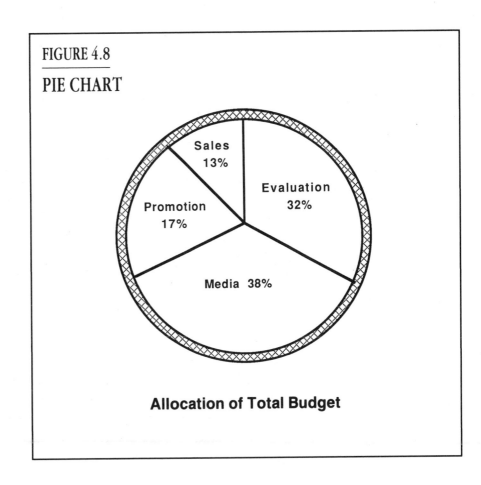

FIGURE 4.8

PIE CHART

Sales 13%

Evaluation 32%

Promotion 17%

Media 38%

Allocation of Total Budget

Line Graphs

A line graph shows points on two dimensions. Usually the vertical dimension represents some amount such as dollars or volume. The horizontal dimension is time. A horizontal line connects the dots or points in time. The most frequent use for a line graph is to show some kind of change over time. A line graph is good for a trend analysis, such as a comparison of prices or sales over time.

Bar Graph

A bar graph is similar in format to a line graph except it depicts units rather than points. For example, the vertical may represent dollars or volume. The horizontal, however, would represent companies, brands, or population segments. You might use a bar graph to compare the consumption patterns of three different segments of your target audience or the dollars spent on advertising by all the various competitors.

There are a number of variations on the basic bar graph. The bars may be drawn as three dimensional units to give the graph more of a feeling of quantity and scale. By drawing bars above and below the horizontal line, you can depict positive and negative data. While most bar graphs illustrate a point in time, they can also be used to show trends over time just like a line graph.

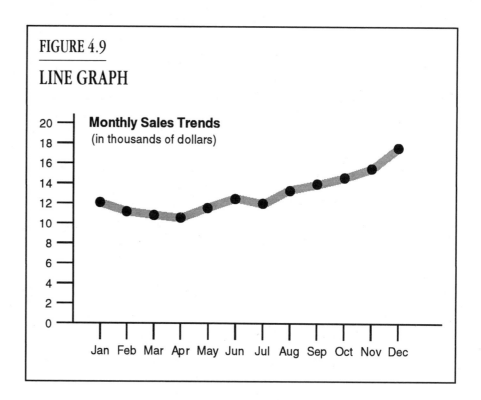

FIGURE 4.9

LINE GRAPH

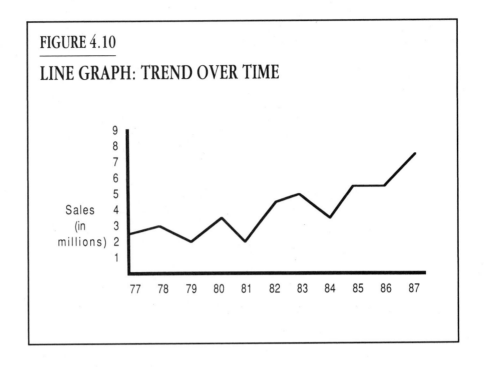

FIGURE 4.10

LINE GRAPH: TREND OVER TIME

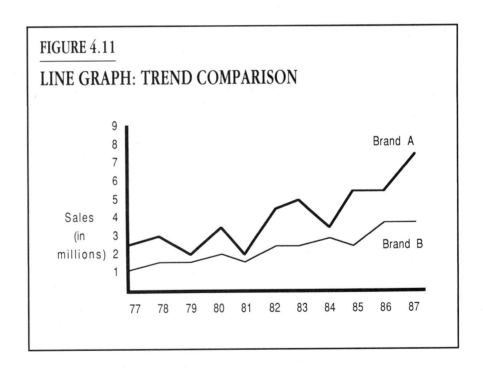

FIGURE 4.11

LINE GRAPH: TREND COMPARISON

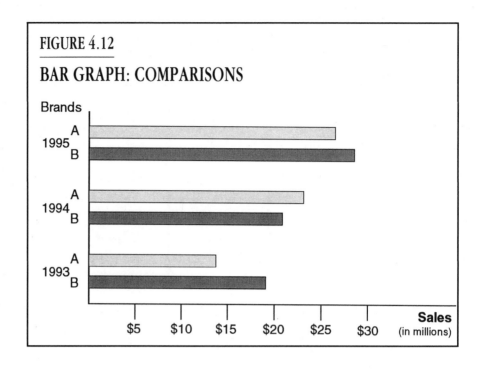

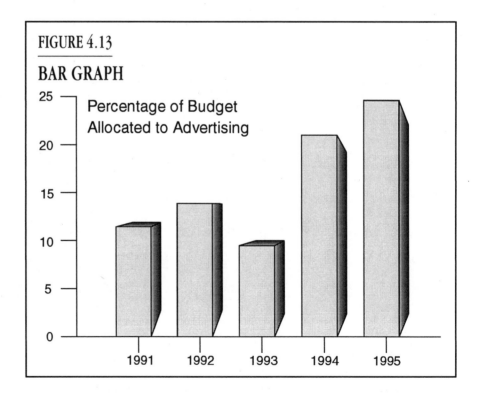

Three dimensional bar graphs can be used to depict the relationship of three elements. The vertical is usually a discrete unit such as brands. Width and depth can be used to indicate dollars, quantity, or measurements.

Plots

A matrix is used to plot relative positions. A scattergram, which plots where various research responses fall, is a type of matrix. A perceptual map is another. To build a matrix, select two different dimensions or measurements and locate one on the vertical and one on the horizontal. Frequently these will be measures that go from low (left and bottom sides) to high (right and top sides). In other words, you're comparing the relative position of things on a two-dimensional scale.

For example, you may want to plot how the target audience sees your brand. You are concerned with the dimensions of quality and price. After asking respondents to rate your product on quality and price, you plot their responses and try to discern a pattern. You will have developed a scattergram which, in this case, shows Brand Y to be perceived as high in both quality and price.

You can do the same type of analysis for your product and the competition. Average the ratings for your product and then plot it, then average the ratings for all your competitors and plot them. A fancy name for this type of evaluation is a perceptual map. It can express research results used to develop a positioning strategy for a brand. It can also be used for showing flavor profiles of competing brands.

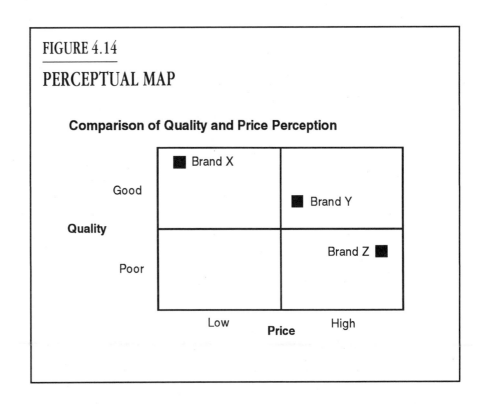

FIGURE 4.14

PERCEPTUAL MAP

Comparison of Quality and Price Perception

Often this type of matrix will be divided in half on both the horizontal and vertical dimensions. This gives quadrants that represent high and low for each of the two dimensions and makes it easier to see relative brand positions.

Pictographs

A variation on many of the previous types of charts and graphs is a pictograph. A pictograph is typically a pie, line, or bar graph that represents the elements with a symbolic graphic. It makes the chart more graphic and more visually interesting.

For example, to express market share for a beer, you might draw a keg and then cut it into sections representing the various percentages of market share. Likewise, to express volume sales for your competition on a bar chart, you let stacks of beer kegs represent different levels of sales volumes.

Pictographs can be used to illustrate seasonality and time of year, maps, weighting strategies, timing strategies, or target audience and media use characteristics. Anything that can be illustrated symbolically can be used to construct a pictograph.

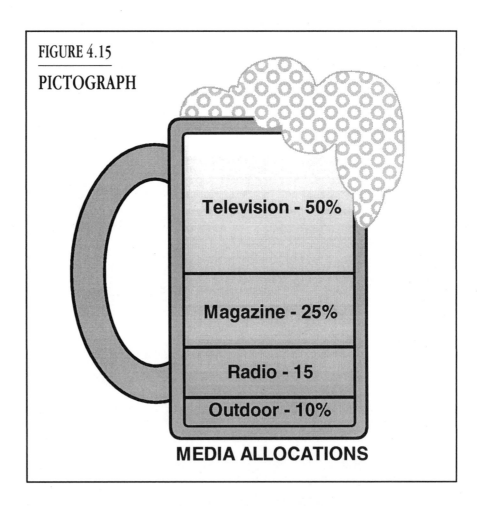

FIGURE 4.15

PICTOGRAPH

Television - 50%

Magazine - 25%

Radio - 15

Outdoor - 10%

MEDIA ALLOCATIONS

PRODUCTION

Charts, graphs, and diagrams are usually drawn by an artist, although computer graphics is rapidly taking over this field. If you are doing it by hand, use India ink and a good technical pen. Words should be professionally lettered or typeset. Typically the art and type are "pasted up" and then photostatted for a clean, professional look. Color can be added using markers or adhesive acetate, tinted sheets of thin plastic that can be easily cut and shaped, for such things as pies in a pie chart and bars in a bar chart.

Labels

Label all charts, tables, and graphs, especially when you are presenting several charts and tables. If you forget labels, the audience will soon start asking themselves, "Which one is this?" The title needn't be long, but it should be descriptive. Also, make sure the "measurements" are clearly labeled. "Sales" isn't enough. Is it sales in dollars, or in units? If in units, which units? When showing years, abbreviate '90, '95. Keep the amount of writing to a minimum.

Design Tricks

There are a number of tricks to designing charts and graphs. To dramatize your point, fill an area with your biggest value. To downplay importance, do the opposite. For example, you can "explode" a section of a pie chart. That means one section is bigger than the scale of the chart and, because of the use of perspective in the illustration, seems to be moving toward the viewer. The larger section gets emphasized whether it is larger proportionally or not because the remainder of the pie is scaled back.

> Label all charts, tables, and graphs

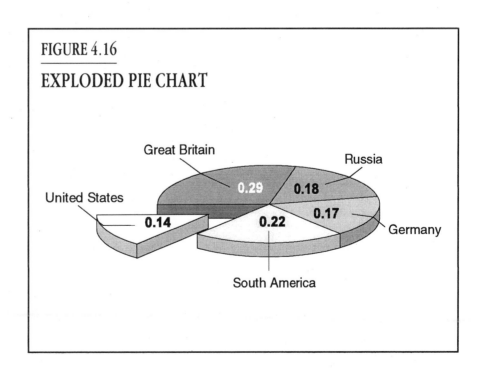

FIGURE 4.16

EXPLODED PIE CHART

If you want to emphasize a gain in a line chart, spread out the vertical dimension and pull in the horizontal. The peaks and valleys appear to be higher. Likewise if you want to de-emphasize a gain, spread out the horizontal dimension and pull in the vertical. This appears to flatten the peaks and valleys.

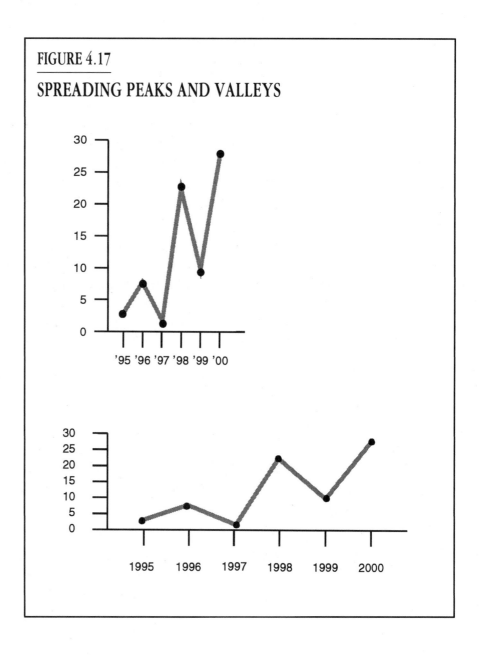

FIGURE 4.17

SPREADING PEAKS AND VALLEYS

Collapsed categories can simplify and dramatize data. You may have collected data year by year for twenty years; if you show that in a line chart with twenty points, it will be awfully busy. It will be much easier to scan if you show ten two-year periods. If the changes are significant, you might want to just show five four-year periods. The simpler it gets, the easier it is to understand.

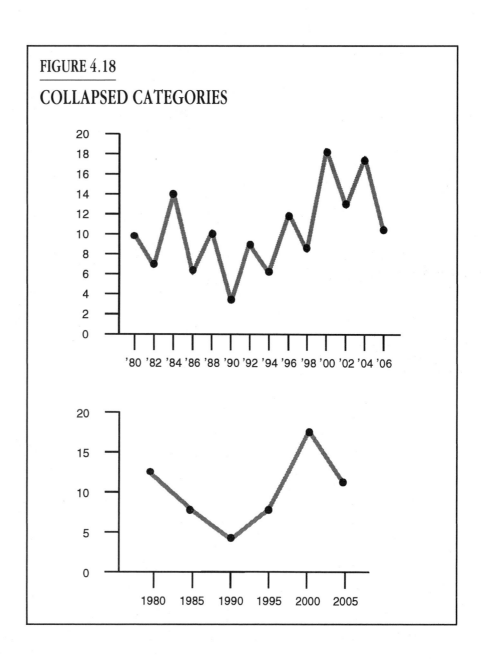

FIGURE 4.18

COLLAPSED CATEGORIES

FIGURE 4.19

SAMPLE DATA IN UNITS AND PERCENT

Data in Units

Units Sold	Market	Percentage of Total
500,000	Men	50%
200,000	Women	20%
300,000	Children	30%

Data in Percentages

Year	Units Sold	Change (in units)	Change (in percentages)
1994	500,000	+ 50,000	10%
1995	550,000	+ 100,000	16%
1996	650,000	- 50,000	8%
1997	600,000		

There are many ways to handle data. You can talk about a change in sales volume in terms of market share, where the units are likely to be small, or in terms of unit volume or dollars, where the numeric units are probably larger. If you want to dramatize the change, then depict the dimension that has the biggest numeric difference. To de-emphasize the change, pick the unit with the smallest numeric values.

You can also talk about actual change—"$3 million this year compared to $2.5 million last year"—or you can depict relative differences—"a change of 17%." A change from $2.5 million to $5 million is a $2.5 million actual increase, but it can also be described as a 100% change or a doubling of the previous value. (Note that a change that doubles, such as from 2% to 4%, is a 100% change. Don't confuse it with the two percentage point increase.) Relative change usually has more impact than unit or actual change because the numeric values seem to be higher. All of these confusing-sounding percentages are much easier to understand if you depict them visually.

I *See* What You Mean

It is possible to have too many visuals and create a visual overload for your audience, but, in most cases, the problem is too few visuals. Generally, the more visuals you use to reinforce your key points and visualize important information, the easier your presentation will be to understand. Remember: when someone understands something you're telling them, they'll say "I *see* what you mean."

CHAPTER 5

Orchestrating the Presentation

KEY POINTS

✎ The dilemma: use the experts or use the naturals?

✎ Emergencies: anything that can go wrong, will

✎ Practices and rehearsals: present ''on automatic''

✎ Find the balance between precision and spontaneity

Once you have outlined your message and prepared your visuals, it's time to think about the actual presentation. The presentation itself can be complex and will require good stage management. While the success of your message depends upon how well you highlight your key points, the success of your presentation depends on attention to details. You want your audience to remember your key points—not audiovisual fiascos.

ROLES

There are a number of roles involved in a presentation. One of the first decisions to be made in planning the actual presentation is to decide who will do what.

EXHIBIT 5.1

DETAILS AND ARRANGEMENTS

Putting on a campaign presentation is like putting on a play. It's a complicated effort. Just a few of the details you have to consider include:

- Who says what and when do they say it?
- Who sits where?
- What props are needed?
- What is needed for staging the presentation—tables, an easel, a podium, a blackboard?
- Will the audience be able to hear and see?
- Is a microphone needed? If so, what kind? Wireless? Lapel?
- Can you adjust the lights? Who will handle the lighting?
- Who handles the visuals?
- How about equipment—will you need a slide projector, tape player, VCR? Who will provide these? Who will run them?

COORDINATING

In presentations that include audiovisuals and more than one presenter, one person should be responsible for logistics. If the highest-ranking person presenting doesn't want to handle presentation logistics, a presentation coordinator should be appointed. If this person is several ranks below the key presenters, things can be awkward. To solve this, the senior person must make it clear to all those involved that the coordinator is responsible for presentation logistics and decisions.

This appointment is important for several reasons. First, it will insure proper arrangements are made. The senior person will probably be too preoccupied with more important things than extension cords and easels. Second, the presentation coordinator can get the senior person's input upfront, avoiding a lot of last-minute changes. Third, because the coordinator is answering directly to the senior presenter, other presenters will be more receptive to the coordinator's direction.

Ideally the coordinator should be someone who has been involved in the initial planning of the presentation. If this is not possible, the coordinator should definitely be appointed before audiovisuals are started as this will help insure a consistent look for all visuals.

The senior presenter should pick the other presenters and inform them of their roles. In large organizations, this can be a highly political decision. In new business pitches, it often indicates who the account team will be should the presentation be successful.

If you are a junior person who must coordinate more senior people, you may want to write the first several memos (regarding deadlines for the visuals, rehearsals, and so forth) over the signature of the key management person who appointed you. Obviously, because you are working closely with the senior management person, he or she will need to see the memo before it goes out.

CASTING

Who says what often depends on the type of presentation. In a pitch for new business, the senior people plus at least one person who will be on the account team should be on stage. This will probably be the account executive or the day-to-day contact person. When Metropolitan Structures Leasing Company of Chicago plans a presentation it brings along the people who will actually work on the project plus a senior executive to show that it takes the client seriously.

An outside consulting agency has only one thing to sell: personal talent. It's only natural to showcase the best people. A frequent client complaint, however, is that "once they got the account, we never saw the people who made the pitch and really impressed us." This potentially negative reaction can be prevented with the right explanation up front. In the opening remarks, the president or senior person should explain what his and the other presenters' roles would be on this account. For example, the senior people generally review all major brand recommendations, sit in on brainstorming sessions for the brand, and review all major creative recommendations. This activity goes on behind the scenes and unless the client is told about them, they will not realize how involved the senior management people are.

It should be made clear if senior people will not be available on a day-to-day basis. Some agency people even turn this "absence" into a positive by saying something like, "I'm sure you would rather have us spend our time thinking and guiding the work on your account than flying back and forth on a plane."

Showcase the best people

PRESENTING

Speakers

The most important decision in presenting is casting the speakers. Sometimes the decision is made on the basis of who knows the most about the plan; other times it is based on who is the best speaker. Each person has a different style and different people work comfortably with different media and in different settings.

Also keep in mind who's going to attend the presentation. Don't bring along too many people if the presentation will be informal or small. Try not to outnumber them.

EXHIBIT 5.2

SELECTING THE SPEAKERS

When you select speakers, consider these criteria:

- All presenters should be familiar with the subject, which means they have been involved long before presentation day
- They should enjoy presenting and be good at it
- They should be compatible with the personality of the client
- Some presenters do better before small rather than large groups

---

Styles

There are many acceptable presentation styles. Some people are thoughtful, low key, precise. Some are funny. Others are so excited about their material that they move through it like a whirlwind, pulling the audience along with them and leaving everyone breathless.

The personality of the speaker determines which style is best. Joe Plumeri, president of investment firm Smith Barney Shearson, says "I never give a speech, I give a chat." The best style is always a natural one. For example, a flamboyant creative should not be forced to give a methodical analysis of the strategy. Leave that to the analytical MBA type.

A secondary concern is using a variety of styles that complement the material and one another. The situation analysis might be given by someone who has a serious, businesslike demeanor. The creative is often presented by someone who can make a fine art of excitement. The change of pace will help maintain attention and keep the audience alert.

There are two rules for choosing your presenters and sometimes they conflict. The first rule is let the people who did it do it. Confidence and credibility come from knowledge of the material. For most people, presenting is a reward, a form of recognition as well as a chance to hear first-hand feedback. Letting those who did the work present is a great motivation tool.

The second rule is use your best presenters. It helps to have specialists to answer questions, but if the media person is Dudley Dull let someone else breathe life into the numbers. The ability to present is a special skill just like the ability to do lettering or a beautiful comp. You don't let the media person do the flow chart, so why assume that he or she has to do the presentation? If you have a problem with a key player who can't or won't present, or one who might create a personality conflict with the client, let someone else in that area do it.

Learning to Present

Presenting is a skill and some people are just naturally good at it. Others aren't—but they can learn if they really make an effort. People who are good at presentation often have some drama or debate training in their background. They like to get up in front of an audience. But even people who like to speak to an audience may admit to getting nervous, so nervousness isn't necessarily an indicator of presentation skills.

Some people who should be presenters say they don't like to get up in front of an audience when, in fact, the real problem is simply that they haven't done it very much. The solution to that is simple—lots of mini-presentations in the office. Confidence comes from experience.

Tom Hagan learned to present at Campbell-Ewald where there were usually six to eight people working on a creative project and often more than one team. "Although the creatives rarely presented to the client, they did present their work through the strata of creative and account management before the work was approved for presentation to clients." Hagan explained that, "these intermediate steps were very important and tense because the management audiences were expert and knew the situation inside and out."

Hagan also points to pressure as a factor in honing presentation skills. "When it came time to make the group's presentation, we never knew who in the group might be called on to stand up, sing, and dance. The creative group head might do it. Or the group head, who was responsible for training his/her people, might turn, at the last minute, to the newest kid in the group and turn the presentation over to that individual. Gulp! You had to be ready at all times. You had to understand all facets of the project. And you had to sell it because the group was depending on you. It was great practice."

Problem Presenters

Then there are people who think they are good presenters but they are not. They can't stick to the outline; their comments wander; or they use a distracting nervous gesture. They may know more than anyone in the room about their area, but it's more than anyone wants to hear. These people need to be given a strict outline and an even stricter time allotment—and they have to be forced to practice in front of the rest of the team. If they go over time or move away from the outline, they don't present anymore, period. This is a discipline problem that requires the attention of someone senior who has the power to enforce discipline.

Problem speakers *can* improve. Chapter Seven, "Delivering Your Message," will discuss more of these speaking problems as well as self-improvement techniques to correct them.

Confidence

Most people, whatever their personal style, can become presenters. It takes work, it takes self-knowledge, and it takes practice. Most people who are good

Most people can be
good presenters

presenters are conscious of themselves. They know how they look, they practice their mannerisms and gestures, and they rehearse smiles and thoughtful looks. Rather than a form of affected self-consciousness, however, this is self-confidence. Confidence comes from knowing you look good, knowing your material thoroughly, and practicing—lots of practicing.

SETTING

The setting speaks, too

The location of the presentation is extremely important because it affects the tone of the presentation. There's a big difference between an auditorium, a classroom, a hotel room, a conference room, and a waiting area in an airport—although important presentations have been made in all these places.

The environment communicates a message of its own, and that message may be difficult to override with your presentation. Sometimes you have no control over where a presentation takes place, however. If you need an answer immediately from the client, you present at his or her convenience, wherever that may be.

QUESTIONS OF TURF

It's a question of turf—yours or theirs. Generally you have to go to "the big ones—they control the environment." They are testing you on their turf, and it can be unsettling and awkward. John Grant once presented to a regional client that had also asked a rather arrogant New York agency head to present. The client "had an in-house viewing room with beautiful wall covering," Grant explains, but the New Yorker used masking tape on the wall and ruined it. As you would expect, he didn't get the account.

If you have never presented at the clients' office, a simple call to the clients' office manager can help you work out details and arrangements ahead of time and give you a good idea what you can and can't do.

If it's your conference room, you have more control over arrangements and equipment. Because you have home advantage, it's easier for you to impress your prospective client with your environment. On the other hand, it may put your client in a psychological position of less control. If you meet at the clients' office, they control the space, and they may feel flattered that you would come to them even though the trip may be expensive and a lot more trouble.

RECONNOITER

The importance of the environment can't be overemphasized. Check out everything. Bring duplicates of everything you can. If you want to modify the room, ask for permission. If you can't get in ahead of time, think of a creative way to do it in the presence of your audience. Or think of a logical reason to see the room first.

Check out the room's physical logistics ahead of time. Know the power source, the lighting and heating controls, the ventilation. At a major presentation at Hilton Head, one agency using a multimedia show suddenly found themselves without power. At first they thought it was a power failure, but on checking they discovered that their power came from an extension cord run to a neighboring room. It had been disconnected by a maid who was vacuuming.

Rooms are not always designed for presentations. Conference rooms may only be set up for meetings around a table. Classrooms can be dreadful if the chairs are nailed down and the lights can't be adjusted. Ideally you need a relatively large space in front for a staging area. You need someplace for the audience to sit, preferably at tables, and everyone should have an unobstructed view of the speaker.

Size Implications

There is an interaction between the size of the room, the number of participants, and the type of presentation you are planning. Slides, for example, can be used almost anywhere, especially if you have a zoom lens and a light plain wall or, of course, a screen. Boards, on the other hand, can only be seen for about 20 feet. In a small group, boards are fine. If you are presenting in a large room or auditorium, then slides, with their enlargement capability, are probably best. If you're in a small room, you'll probably be projecting to a screen image of approximately 3 to 4 feet. If you're in a large room, you may need a screen image of 10 to 12 feet.

PRESENTATION SETUPS

Seating

A traditional presentation setup usually has a staging area where the presenters speak, and sometimes sit. They face tables where the client representatives sit. If the company has support people who are not presenters, they are likely to sit in the wings where they are available for questions. A "power setting" will be arranged so that the primary speakers are talking directly to Mr. Big, the most influential decision maker in the room. However, this arrangement may unnecessarily foster an "us versus them" feeling. To downplay this potentially adversarial context, some presenters try to mix everyone around the table or tables. This establishes camaraderie and gives the feeling that everyone is part of the same team. The presenters either speak from their chairs or they sit near the front so they can stand up and move to the front easily. Always have the president of the presenting company sit next to the president of the client company to answer questions.

Staging

One important part is planning where the speakers stand in relation to both the visuals and the audience. Good speakers refer to the visuals. They use them as notes. They must see them to work from them, so you don't want the speakers between the visuals and the audience. If the visuals are behind the speakers, they will have to turn their backs to the audience in order to use them. They may also block the audience's view.

One solution is to use a "presentation triangle" in which presenters stand opposite the visuals and both face the audience. If you're using slides, have the presenters positioned on either side of the screen. With boards, the speaker may be in the middle with the easels on either or both sides.

Lighting

You may want to set different levels of lighting for different parts of the room, or you may need to darken all or part of the room for showing slides. Unless a room is designed for presentations, you might have to improvise. You may have to bring a podium light, for example, if variable lighting isn't possible.

Good presentation style, however, demands that you maintain eye contact, so try to avoid turning off the lights entirely. Out of years of habit, we have learned that when the lights go out, it's time for bed. Susanne Townsend, in an article in *Advertising Age,* calls turning out the lights "a bullet to the brain." Once the lights go off, attention tends to wander and you may find your audience asleep—particularly if you are presenting after lunch.

Modern meeting rooms often have ceiling spotlights that can be di-

---

EXHIBIT 5.3

PLANNING THE STAGING

Ask these questions when you plan the arrangement of the stage area:

- Where do the tables or podium go?
- Where do the presenters sit? How do they get from their seats to their speaking positions?
- What's the choreography for the change of speakers?
- Where do the screen and/or easels go?
- What happens to the old boards when you move on to the next ones? Where will you put them? Who moves them?
- Who turns off the lights? Who advances the slides?

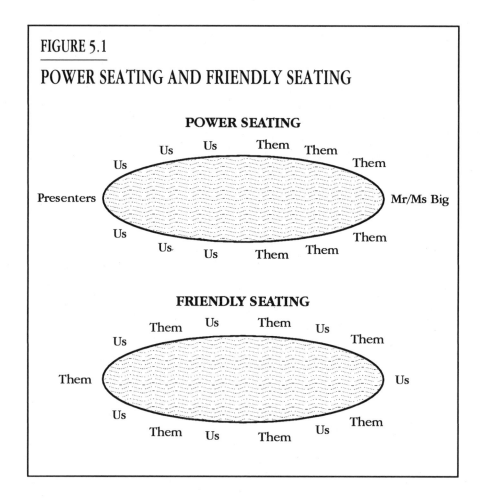

rected down on the audience but still leave the screen relatively dark. Generally these provide enough light to take notes and keep people awake.

ARRANGEMENTS

STAGE MANAGER

A presentation needs a stage manager to think through these details ahead of time. He or she plays a slightly different role than the coordinator. The coordinator administrates and manages while the stage manager takes charge of all the tiny details that can ruin a presentation if overlooked. Obviously the coordinator can handle the role of stage manager, but you might consider letting a separate person do it.

As the campaign develops and you practice presenting its various sections, most of the details will emerge. Will you need masking tape or push pins to attach visuals to a wall? Do you need duct tape to cover extension

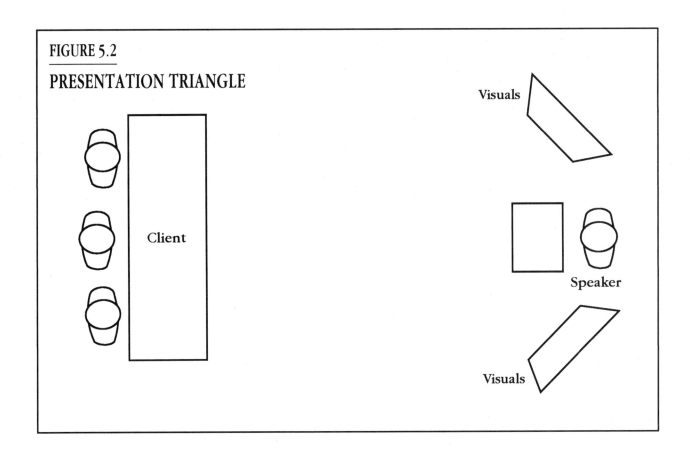

FIGURE 5.2

PRESENTATION TRIANGLE

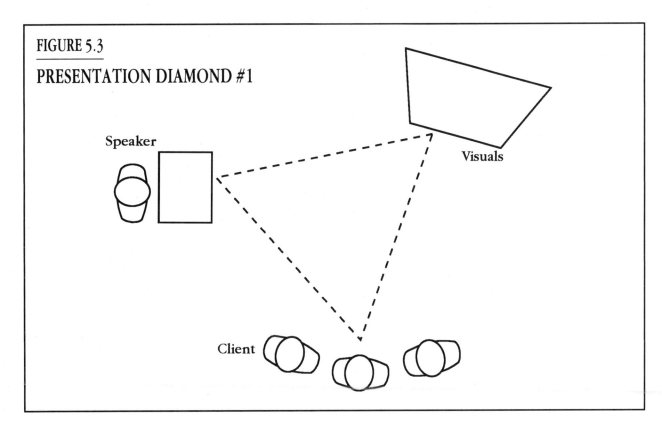

FIGURE 5.3

PRESENTATION DIAMOND #1

FIGURE 5.4

PRESENTATION DIAMOND #2

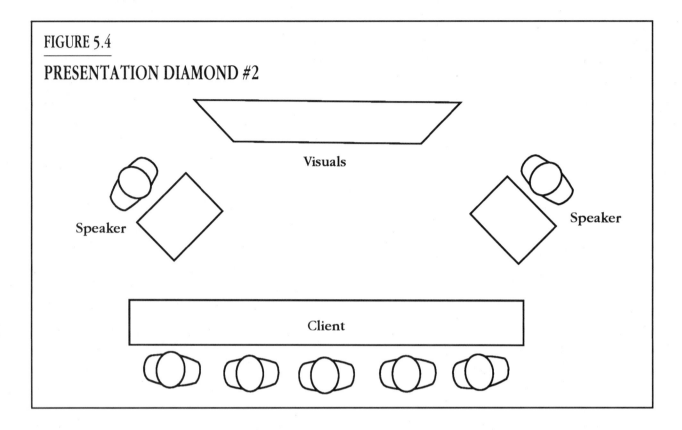

cords strung along the floor? How about remote controls for the projectors and three-prong adapter plugs?

Regardless of where you meet, your stage manager must reconnoiter the room ahead of time and figure out what needs to be done or provided. Is there outside noise? Can it be controlled or is it too loud to ignore? How does the heating and ventilation system work? Can the windows be opened? Where are the outlets and the light switches? Is there a screen? A blackboard? Can you tack things on the wall?

Reconnoiter the presentation room ahead of time

ANALYZING NEEDS

If you are on their turf, you have to provide everything that is not otherwise available and you may have to improvise and make do. Prepare for all eventualities. Anticipate bulb failure, wrong plug adapters, missing extension cords, etc. You can count on it: As soon as the slide projector is turned on, the bulb will blow out. If it's lunch hour or break and the AV person is gone, it can take a long time to get the presentation back on track.

Checklists

An important function of the stage manager is to make the *master checklist* noting all of the details so that none are forgotten during the confusion before the presentation. (A good sample checklist can be found in the appendix.)

EXHIBIT 5.4

THINGS TO KNOW BEFORE YOU PRESENT

Before the presentation begins, reconnoiter the room, talk to the management staff, and be ready to troubleshoot.

1. Where is the temperature control? Once the room fills up with people, the temperature can change 5 to 8 degrees and you may need to adjust it.

2. Know how to reach instantly facilities and technical staff such as an electrician and the supervisor or manager.

3. If equipment is provided or rented, know how to get hold of technical people quickly if an equipment failure occurs.

4. Find out what will be going on in adjoining rooms during your presentation. If you are booking a room, arrange that there will be no music next door.

5. If the room has piped in sound, find out how to turn it off.

6. If you are planning a formal presentation to a large group and you don't want interruptions, have at the door someone who knows everyone, to take messages.

7. Make sure the telephone operator who is on the board during both practices and presentations knows who is in your group (both agency and client) and where you are.

8. Make sure there is enough room for clients to be comfortable, a place for people to put their coats, set their briefcases down, and so on.

The stage manager may also be responsible for "dressing" the room. Do you need pencils and notepads? Who will provide them? How about coffee?

Many of the checklist details relate to the media and visuals. Check the projector to make sure that a power cord and remote advance are included in the case. Check the lens—zoom lenses are most useful because they can adjust to various size rooms. Always use a projector with automatic focus unless all your slides are perfectly focused. You may even want a backup projector. Don't forget converter plugs so your three-prong projector can plug into a two-prong outlet.

If you are using an easel, make sure you have the base that your boards will sit on—some easels are set up for using newspaper pads like flip charts. If you want to use a blank pad and develop the visuals as you go, make sure you have a pad and the kind of easel that will hold it. If you need pegs or any kind of pieces for the easels, bring extras. Try out the easels to see if the base is wide enough for all the boards you will be using. Also make sure it is sturdy enough. Presentations have gone crazy when the telescoping legs on the easel slowly begin to collapse or the easel itself suddenly tips over backwards.

You probably would think to check for a blackboard when you reconnoiter the room, but don't forget to bring chalk, push pins, and markers.

Some conference rooms now use write-on walls that take a different kind of erasable marker. Better check it out and be prepared. If you are using an overhead projector, don't forget pens or grease pencils that write on acetate. Most regular felt tips and ink pens won't show on overhead transparencies.

Name Tags and Cards

Do you need name tags or name cards? If you are presenting to a long-time client, you probably don't need name tags. If you're dealing with a new client or making a spec presentation, name identification is important. Names tend to get lost in introductions and no one should get anyone's name wrong. That can happen easily in the confusion and tension of a major presentation; to be on the safe side, every presenter should have a name tag and all the client representatives should have name cards on the table in front of them. A roster of your company's names may also be handed out to the client. Some people dislike name tags. Consequently, rather than embarrassing a potential client, or worse, having him tell you "no thanks," use name cards if they are seated at a table. People like name cards as much as they dislike name tags.

Emergencies

In addition to the master checklist, there should also be a *checklist for emergencies.* Think through not what has happened in the practice sessions, but what didn't happen. In other words the whole team should brainstorm on what could go wrong and then develop a list of emergency supplies. The common emergencies involve bulbs that go out in projectors and cords that aren't long enough. Obviously if you are using media equipment you need replacement bulbs as well as extension cords for power and the remote advance.

Understudies

There's a personal side to emergencies, too. What if one of the presenters gets sick? Is there someone else on the team who can fill in? Every presenter should have an understudy, someone who knows that section well enough to be able to step in at the last minute.

REHEARSALS

Rehearsals bring the presenters together with the content and the presentation format. Successful presenters have found that their success is often proportional to the amount of preparation and rehearsal time devoted to the presentation.

THE PRACTICE SCHEME

Most people get ready for a presentation by first practicing over and over by themselves, then into a recorder, then in front of one or several colleagues, perhaps in front of a videotape camera, before the other presenters, and finally before a review group of senior executives.

Individual Practice

Know it so well that you can present "on automatic"

The first level of practice is by yourself, on your own. You have to go over it enough to know your material. There is no shortcut. You must know the content of the message so well that you can present it no matter what. Dancers call this "muscle memory"—even if your mind goes blank, your body knows the part so well that you can continue. If you are distracted by a noisy fan or radiator, your body knows the message. Even if the projector breaks down or the boards get left in a taxi, you know the message well enough to present without the visual cues.

A good way for an individual to practice alone is to use a tape recorder and record each of the run-throughs. Listen to it, analyze the awkward spots, note the points where the logic gets lost, revise the whole thing and do it again. A presentation is an oral exercise, so the best practice is oral.

Trial Runs

The next stage is to do trial runs section by section before the rest of the team. After the person presenting each section has practiced it alone many times, he or she needs to present it to others to see if it hangs together and makes sense to them.

If the team can't get together to listen to these sections, individual trial runs can be done in front of anyone who is willing to listen. As a matter of fact, people who have not been involved in the planning are sometimes the best audience because they don't know what you are trying to say. They will notice points of confusion. They will also ask questions, often unexpected questions, that best test your Q & A responses.

Next, do a trial run of the entire presentation. Work on introductions, transitions, and choreography, as well as the timing of the entire presentation. Most presentations are under a time limit agreed to by both sides or imposed by the client. It's considered bad form to take more than the allotted time. If the client has given you a deadline, stick to it. To do so, your team may even want to develop a signal to warn each presenter when time is running out and it's time for a wrap-up.

In addition, you may need to be flexible when the actual presentation comes. According to Steve Walker, executive vice president with Equitable Real Estate, "You have to give the clients what they want on their time schedule. If the client has promised you an hour and gives you only 15 minutes when you get there, you have to adapt quickly."

It may take several trial runs before the presentation finally begins to come together. You might rent a conference room somewhere away from the agency for this rehearsal. John Grant describes rehearsing in a hotel room at 4:00 A.M. the morning of a major presentation. "It's like a Broadway opening—you have a real sense of performance."

Try doing the trial run in exactly half the allotted time. One agency executive has experienced a review board that frequently says, "start at the end and tell us the guts first." This can make you focus more tightly on the key points. This is not an unrealistic situation. You may walk into a presentation only to discover that the CEO has to leave for London in 20 minutes. If that's all the time you've got, you either adjust or walk away. Presenters who have been through this inevitably report that the presentation was the best they have ever given.

If time is critical, assign someone on the team to be timekeeper. Plan how long each section should be and have that person keep track during the practices. Develop a set of hand signals that mean "cut" or "speed up." Videotaping may also be used at the time of the trial runs. A videotape can be used to spot any part of the presentation that doesn't work. It's also good to identify personal style problems with the presenters. It's for final polishing and editing.

Rehearsal Formula

A more complicated rehearsal scheme suggests that individuals practice their sections at several times both alone and with a tape recorder. Then schedule several group practices with the whole group, with a video recorder, and a final one before a review board.

Dress Rehearsal

If there is time, the next step is a dress rehearsal in front of an informed and critical audience. Some companies use an in-house review board of senior executives to review the content of the plan and the presentation style. They also deliberately ask tough questions to get the team ready for the Q & A session.

A classic example of what can happen when an agency presents without adequate rehearsal time is the legendary presentation made by Chiat/Day to its long-time client, Apple—and how the agency lost the account in the process. John Sculley, then Apple CEO, noting that the agency's team didn't seem to have it together described it this way: "As each of the Chiat people moved to the front of the room, it seemed as if the presentation had never been rehearsed. People were blowing their lines, losing their places, and apparently speaking over their allotted times." Chiat devoted the first three hours to overall strategy, an analysis of the market, and the media plan before ever getting to the creative point, the actual advertising. "As the actual creative presentation involved 150 pieces of creative work, it strained the presentation abilities of the team to manage the timing and explanation of the work. (Copywriter Steve) Hayden began rushing through much of the creative because the agency was clearly running out of time. Indeed, I noticed that he began skipping over several pieces of creative instead of presenting it all.''

PRACTICE SUGGESTIONS

Practice time is difficult for busy people to schedule, but it is very important. Try recording solo practice sessions and then circulate those tapes among team members. Schedule group rehearsals during noncompeting times of day like early mornings and evenings. To minimize the interruptions and focus everyone's attention, get away from the office. Some companies will rent a meeting room in a hotel and spirit everyone away for an afternoon or evening.

Practice until you know the material, but don't memorize it. If you practice too much, you run the risk of upsetting the delicate balance between precision and spontaneity. The ideal is to ''talk'' your material convincingly. Remember, a presentation is a ''conversation.'' Good conversationalists don't speak memorized lines—or, if they do, no one knows it.

How many times you practice is up to you, but don't underestimate the need. Ron Hoff says in *Advertising Age,* that a major problem with many presentations is that they are sloppy; the presenters just haven't taken enough pains to get it right. He recommends that you practice your part at least ten times.

> Find the balance between precision and spontaneity

PREPARATION IS THE KEY

Practices and dress rehearsals are critical parts of the preparation for a presentation. But the preparation begins much earlier. It begins with choosing the speakers and the audiovisual media, with reconnoitering the setting and arranging the room, and, most of all, it begins with a complete and thorough checklist.

SECTION III

GIVING THE PRESENTATION

CHAPTER 6

Making the Presentation

KEY POINTS
- ✎ Personality is mirrored in how you speak
- ✎ Conviction is enthusiasm with a focus
- ✎ Visualize yourself doing well
- ✎ Learn to read your audience
- ✎ Techniques for controlling attention

PRESENTATIONS ARE PERFORMANCES

The *American Heritage Dictionary* defines a presentation as a "performance." As Susanne Townsend, a VP-creative director, said in an *Advertising Age* article: "A person stands in front of other persons . . . while the audience remains seated. She begins talking while they remain silent. Eventually she sits down and they react. . . . That's called a performance, and like it or not, a presentation is a performance." Townsend concluded, "Like any other performance, it's a hit or a bomb."

In business, the two major types of communication are the memo or report and the presentation. The first is passive, the second active. The primary difference between the two is that in a presentation the information is animated, brought to life. The animator is the presenter. He or she is basically "performing" the memo or report.

There's a tendency for some to downplay the performance aspects—to assume they can "wing it," however an effective off-the-cuff presentation takes real skill. To be successful presenters, most people must study, outline, organize, and practice. The more important the presentation and the larger the audience, the more they practice. For some people, trying to "wing it" is a way to handle anxiety. It's also generally a sign of laziness or ignorance of good presentation skills. Others simply believe that their ideas are great and will sell themselves regardless of the presentation. Unplanned presentations, like unrehearsed performances, are extremely risky.

The presenter makes the difference in most presentations. An ad agency president explains that most of the presentation content is the same in competing presentations. Media plans are similar, most research findings are similar, and most full-service agencies are similar in operations and methodology. "Given all that," he says, "a good presenter is what makes the difference."

BEFORE THE PRESENTATION

The performance begins before anyone stands up or anything is said. As in a play, most of the work is done before the curtains open.

GETTING READY

The Setup

You start with an empty room. Somehow you, or someone on your team, will need access to the room before the presentation, before the people take their seats. You may want to rearrange the stage area. If it's in a hotel, you may need to have union people do the moving. Work closely on this with the conference or catering director, or the office manager if it's in an office.

The Run-Through

Walk through the presentation in the presentation room. Punch up every slide, show every visual in order. If there is audio, play it at the appropriate places and check the levels. If lights need to be dimmed during the presentation, practice dimming them at the appropriate times. This will insure that

- Everyone knows what to do and when to do it

- Each person knows how to do his job (operate the dimmer, adjust the audio, etc.)

- All the equipment works
- By showing all slides in the run-through, you can make sure they all fit the screen

When the run-through is completed, go back and cue up all the media so they are ready to go at the touch of a button. By now, you should know the answers to the questions and situations raised in Exhibit 5.4. Take another look at it just to be sure.

Socializing

Plan what happens to people before the presentation and as they enter the room. Some companies like to arrange a social event before the formal presentation. Coffee and donuts are a good social lubricant and an informal setting like this can help establish the feeling of teamwork between agency and client. It reduces tension and lets people introduce one another informally. Companies that use this technique recommend having the social event in a different room. First of all, that leaves the presentation room free for set up. In addition, it separates the social part of the presentation from the business part.

There are two primary reasons to socialize before the presentation begins. First, if people know you and like you, they will be more receptive to what you have to say. Second, if you know and like them, you can focus on them rather than on your own nervousness.

If people know you and like you, they will be more receptive

It's only human nature to evaluate on the basis of first impressions—she seems intelligent, he seems self-confident, he seems preoccupied, she's arrogant. A presenter has a better chance of making a positive impression during an informal introduction than during those first nervous seconds behind the lectern. Also, once you start speaking, your audience can immediately focus on what you are saying, rather than making judgments about your style and personality because they have already done that.

So how do you introduce yourself in a natural way to a room full of strangers before a presentation? The "politician's approach" is simply to walk up and shake hands. Some presenters feel this is too stressful, especially if they are already tense and nervous about presenting.

A more relaxed and natural way to introduce yourself before the presentation is to walk around with a "conversation piece" in hand, such as a cartoon—blown up and mounted—an interesting picture, or some other object that is interesting and relevant to the presentation. This object should be relevant to the presentation topic. For example, before one workshop on creative presentations, the leader, who was unknown to the participants, walked around the room showing an old photograph of a formal business meeting in which half of the audience was asleep. Not only was the picture funny, it was relevant. More importantly, it made a statement about the workshop leader—that he had a sense of humor, was warm and friendly, and would be interesting to listen to.

In addition to "warming up" your audience, meeting them beforehand has several advantages for the presenter. The audience won't be filled with complete strangers, which makes the situation more psychologically reassuring. It's now easier to focus on them and their needs instead of on yourself and your butterflies. You have psychological license to be more conversational and less formal.

GIVING THE PRESENTATION

After everyone is seated, the focus moves to each individual presenter as he or she takes the floor. What does a good presenter do? As speech teachers have long known, it's all in the delivery.

INDIVIDUAL STYLE

> Your personality is mirrored in how you speak

Not only is it important to determine the tone of the overall presentation—it's also critical to choose an appropriate tone for your own delivery.

Every person has a unique presentation style; your personality is mirrored in how you speak. You can adopt some general techniques to make presenting easier for you, but it is probably unwise to try to force yourself into some "ideal" style. It's better to be natural, to polish your own personal style, and to build on your personality strengths.

The tone that you set foreshadows the response of your audience. They respond to such things as nervousness, arrogance, hostility, or warmth. You get a feeling "in the gut" when someone starts to speak—and so do they. You know automatically if you like or trust that person—they'll know, too.

Ron Hoff in an *Advertising Age* article on presentations says that if the presenter is nervous, for example, the audience will be uncomfortable. If you are arrogant, the audience will challenge you, but if you are at ease, the audience will more likely be warm and receptive.

It was this betrayal of agency style that may have contributed to Chiat/Day's loss of the Apple account. Former Apple CEO John Sculley says that Chiat/Day showed up with an entourage of seven people, including Chiat and President Lee Clow, all in conservative suits. "I couldn't believe it. Jay, who often dressed in bulky Italian knit sweaters, was suited. Clow, a tall, lanky man with a long beard and dark blond shoulder-length hair, generally would come to Apple in sandals and shorts. Today, he donned a dark blue suit."

The uncomfortable change of style was aggravated by fatigue. The team had driven in a rental van the night before the presentation. "They seemed weary and exhausted, as if they had been living on coffee for a long time. I was later to learn that most of them had been working 16–18 hour days in a near-hysteric state for the past seven weeks to prepare the presentation."

EXHIBIT 6.1

FIRST IMPRESSIONS

Keeping in mind that the audience is extremely judgmental in the beginning, what you do in the first thirty seconds can affect how they will react to your total presentation. Here's what you can do to help insure that this first impression is positive.

1. While you are being introduced, move to the front of your chair with both feet squarely beneath you. If you are holding something that you are not going to take to the lectern, place it on the floor or table now.

2. Stand up in one smooth motion. Don't put a hand on the back of a chair or the table and look like you are climbing out of your seat.

3. Walk to the podium with energy. Pretend that you are receiving an Academy Award for your performance. Don't look at your feet, the clock, or your notes; walk enthusiastically to the lectern for your award.

4. Put a warm smile on your face before you get to the lectern so it's there when you turn toward the audience for the first time.

5. Before you start speaking, make some eye contact, establishing contact with individuals in the audience.

6. Now say something that is warm and friendly and matches your smile.

7. Don't look at your notes during your opening words. (If you want to check that your notes are there and in order, do so before you start to speak.) Nothing lowers perceived credibility more than when a speaker looks at his notes, looks at the audience, and then says how pleased he or she is to be there. "Being pleased" comes from the heart, not from notes.

Enthusiasm

One general principle is to be enthusiastic. Almost without exception, speaking coaches insist that you can't lull or bore your audience into action. You have to leave them excited about your idea, and to do that you have to be excited about it yourself. This is the ingredient that generates millions of dollars in contributions to television preachers. Their enthusiasm for their work is extremely motivating.

Remember, presentations are show business. It is often true that people who are dynamite on stage are quiet in real life—enthusiasm on stage isn't something you can always predict.

Conviction

Conviction contributes to persuasiveness because it builds credibility. Conviction is enthusiasm with a focus, a direction, a specific point of view. If you

**Conviction is enthusiasm
with a focus**

believe, they believe. Susanne Townsend notes that "you are your most powerful weapon when you are most sincere, most enthusiastic, most honest, most involved and most genuinely excited."

Conviction and enthusiasm transcend personal style. Whether you are thoughtful and low key or hyper and highly animated, you still have natural ways to express your enthusiasm for an idea and your belief in it. Analyze your response when someone gives you a present or a compliment. How do you feel and respond? How do they know that you are pleased? What cues do you send? Those cues, which can be identified and practiced, express both conviction and enthusiasm.

Credibility

As mentioned before, the first thing each listener decides is whether he or she likes the speaker. Once this has been decided, they ask if the speaker is telling the truth. "Should I believe him or her?" Keep in mind that liking and believing are two different judgments. There is no question that being liked will aid in being believed, but it doesn't guarantee it.

An audience uses several cues to decide whether to believe the speaker. Does the speaker make good eye contact? Remember the old saying, "Can you look me straight in the eye and say that?" Is the delivery smooth, or is the speaker hesitant and overly cautious in choosing his or her words? This may give the audience the idea that the speaker is too calculating or insincere; that he or she is telling them what they want to hear rather than the way it actually is.

Another aspect of credibility is respect. Speakers who seem patronizing or arrogant appear not to respect their audience. This implies that the speaker is superior and that the audience's viewpoint has little value. The audience responds by counterarguing. The persuasiveness of the speaker is neutralized because the audience will try to find reasons not to believe.

Overreliance on notes can also hurt credibility. If you know what you are talking about, you should not have to rely heavily on notes. Reading word-for-word from a script detracts from your expertise.

MENTAL SELF-IMAGE

There is an old saying that "action follows feeling." If you want to act like a professional, you have to feel like one. As the wizard told the lion in the Wizard of Oz, to develop courage, act as if you already have it. A lot of it is desire. If you really want to be a dynamite presenter, then believe in yourself.

Confidence

Confidence—that's what you need to project. Your appearance reflects your inner state and shows the audience where you are on the confidence scale. To look confident and reduce your anxiety, try these tricks before speaking. Take a

To develop courage, act as if you already have it

deep breath, or better yet, breathe deeply for thirty seconds or so. You will increase the supply of oxygen going to your brain rather than to your feet.

Putting the tip of your tongue against your lower teeth and pushing forward will help stretch the muscles in the back of your mouth, your throat, and the vocal cord area. Tight vocal cords make a person's voice rise up, a clear sign of nervousness. (Obviously you should do this in another room or with your back to the audience since it distorts your facial expression.) Finally, practice your opening lines in your mind.

Dale Carnegie recommends a wonderful technique for thinking yourself into a power position. Imagine that everyone in the room owes you money and that they have all met together to beg you for an extension. Think of yourself as the power in the room—never undertake any presentation imagining defeat or thinking that you are inferior to your audience.

Visualization

Visualize yourself doing well; stage for success

There is a significant body of literature on self-improvement techniques that use visualization. It started with books on skiing and playing tennis that described how you can almost magically improve your technique by creating a mental image of yourself doing this skill well. Visualization has become an important part of the repertoire of most coaches and professional athletes.

If you imagine yourself looking good and making the presentation with ease, you are likely to be a more relaxed and confident presenter. Rehearse in your mind the behavior that you want to achieve. Set your mental stage for success.

Mental Preparation

Most good presenters rely on some kind of system to prepare themselves mentally before making a presentation. Sometimes these are ritual behaviors, some kind of activity or thought process that they used in the past when everything worked well. Because the behavior worked once, they repeat it, hoping for the same success. It may just be a way of dressing—a particular suit or favorite tie. Little things like a tie or some other object may be more like a "good luck charm," but "dressing for success" is always psychologically sound.

MANAGING THE SITUATION

READING THE ROOM

Reading the room means tuning into your audience so well that you know what is going on in their minds. It means knowing when they are attentive, when they are following your logic, and when they aren't listening to you.

EXHIBIT 6.2

BODY LANGUAGE CUES

Body language can tell you a lot about what is going on in the minds of your audience. The following cues mean they are probably going to miss some of what you are saying:

- Are they slumping in their chairs?
- Have they swung their bodies around so they are facing away from you?
- Are they talking among themselves?
- Are they staring at the ceiling or looking out the window?
- Did someone look up or down suddenly?
- Is there a look of disbelief or puzzlement?
- Do you hear nervous coughing or clearing of the throat?
- Are they all caught up in taking notes?
- Are they reading something other than what you are talking about?

Body Language

Read their body language. If people are slumping in their chairs, talking to each other, or staring at the ceiling, you've lost them. If your audience is bent over taking notes, stop and let them catch up. If their heads are down, there's no chance for eye contact, and their minds are concentrating on what you already said rather than what you are getting ready to say.

Changes in body language usually indicate some kind of major internal response. Watch out for folding arms, quizzical expressions, nervous coughing, rapid blinking, and sudden glances up or down. You may have said something that caused them discomfort or disagreement. What was it? Make a mental note and be ready for a question later on.

One of the senior presenters should watch the expressions of the audience members to see if they are bored or if more explanation is needed. A creative director once tried to explain an animation technique to clients. Seeing that they didn't understand, he stopped the presentation, went down the hall, and got a sample reel to demonstrate the special effect he was explaining. Even if you don't want to interrupt the presentation to provide this additional explanation, the "monitor" should note the need for it and be prepared to elaborate on that point in the question-and-answer period.

Anticipate Response

Careful observation of your audience will give you insight into their response. You can often spot problem areas, points of confusion, misunderstanding, and disagreement by watching their faces and body language. Use

Learn to read the audience

that as a cue to switch gears, pause, redefine or rephrase, or restate the logic of the argument. If the audience is small and the tone of the presentation is relatively informal, then stop and react. Ask, "Is this clear? Does it make sense? Does anyone interpret that differently?"

While these questions can help clarify what has been said and help diffuse potential problems resulting from misinterpretations, they can also bring up totally new areas. Occasionally these new areas can put a completely new perspective on your presentation—one that could even make your recommendations off the mark. You may be thrown by this, but it's better to have a chance to adjust than to have your whole plan rejected without knowing why or having the opportunity to respond.

Don't Overreact

Don't overreact to your audience. There will always be someone who looks bored or someone who fidgets. Someone who appears to be pouting and displeased might have been reprimanded by a boss just before the meeting, or perhaps had a fight with a spouse that morning. The fidgeter might be one of those people whose muscles tighten up when they sit too long. You can't take responsibility for everything your audience is thinking about or doing.

Some professional presenters (though they are a minority) say you shouldn't try to read the audience at all. If you are well-prepared, have good visuals, and are well-organized, then you have done all that you can do. They contend that if you concentrate too much on the audience you will lose your natural rhythm and confidence in what you are saying and then your presentation will really suffer.

The less experienced you are at presenting, the more you should stick to what you have practiced. Then after each presentation ask people, particularly those who will give you an honest critique, for feedback. As you gain confidence and experience in presenting, you can begin to experiment with diverting from your outline when you think you have an audience problem.

CONTROLLING ATTENTION

Everyone's attention wanders. You'll never have their attention 100% of the time. But when attention wanders, your audience will miss something. Since most presentations are scripted to build point by point to some logical climax, missing a point can weaken the logic of the proposal. Attention tends to wander in the middle of the presentation, during discussions of theoretical concepts, after lunch and on Friday afternoons. Plan for these natural situations and build in techniques to overcome them.

Suspense is a great technique for maintaining interest. If you are building up to some major unveiling, work in a little suspense to intensify the attention. For example, if you are recommending a new promotion that

---

EXHIBIT 6.3

HOW TO PULL THEM BACK

If you are convinced you're losing your audience's attention, there are several ways to pull them back and reconnect.

1. Stop talking. The silence will be deadening. Start speaking again by saying something like "of all the points presented so far, the most important is _____. Don't you agree?"

2. Pick up the pace. Often a drifting audience is actually drowning in a sea of facts and figures. If you think this is the case, skip over some of the supporting details, hit the major points, and then ask for questions. If you moved too fast, they will ask you to explain, defend, etc., which means they are again with you.

3. Become more animated. Bang the lectern to emphasize a point, raise your voice—"Never, never should we let our competitors steal our shelf position!"

4. Move. Get out from behind the lectern, walk up to someone on the first row and ask him if what you said makes sense.

5. Be more entertaining. Do an imitation of a consumer, a buyer, or a competitor by talking in a funny voice or exaggerated tone.

6. Ask a question. "Can someone recap what we have covered so far?" Don't actually put someone on the spot for an answer, but let the question hang in the air and look at a few people. Thinking they might actually be called upon will generally scare them awake.

7. Call a break, especially if the presentation has been going on for over an hour. Ask everyone to stand up for a few seconds. Tell them the good part is coming up and you want them to be wide awake.

---

includes trips to Hawaii, show hula dancers and surfers in between the tables and graphs.

Attention wanders any time you are talking about theories, abstractions, numbers, or generalizations. The solution is to be as specific as possible. Follow the important general statements with examples or anecdotes.

Eye contact is a key to commanding attention. Raising or lowering the voice, pausing, and moving from one place to another are all ways to demand and direct the audience's attention. Pointing is another useful technique, as is any kind of action, such as piling pounds of computer printouts on the table during the research discussion. Media directors, who have a really difficult section to present because of all the numbers, have been known to wave copies of the magazines to illustrate the buy. In a presentation to the Colorado Tourism Board, a media planner donned sunglasses when talking about the summer media blitz and wound a wool scarf around her neck when talking about the winter schedule.

Finally, plan in advance how to handle interruptions. Paul Saunders, president and CEO of Saunders Systems Corporation, an international management consulting company, warns that some upper level managers may arrive late or leave early. If the decision-maker arrives a few minutes late, start over; if he or she arrives 20 or 30 minutes late, summarize what he or she has missed; if he or she arrives near the end of the presentation, don't regroup, just proceed. Saunders also advises that if the decision maker leaves early, don't let down on the presentation. Someone else from the client's company will still be paying attention and you should continue to show enthusiasm for your work.

HANDLING THE "STUFF"

Equipment

Everyone on the presentation team should know how to operate the equipment being used. If you are using slides, know how to operate the projector, hook up the dissolve unit, focus and advance the slides, and change the bulb. If you are using video, you need to know the difference between 1/2-inch and 3/4-inch formats and how to hook the player up to the monitor. Of course, you need to know how to insert the cassette and where the play, fast forward, pause, and reverse buttons are.

An overhead projector is easy to use, but you still need to practice using it in order not to fumble. Nothing is more distracting and unimpressive than upside down or backwards transparencies on an overhead projector. For all projected visuals you need to know how to set up the projector, focus it, and fill the screen without any of the typically novice errors like keystoning. Keep your projector's lens level with the screen; don't use an ashtray to tilt the projector because that distorts the image, i.e. creates "keystoning."

An example of overdoing it occurred when the Hal Riney agency made a pitch for the MasterCard account and brought in a team of nine presenters and so many props and visual aids that take-down and pack-up took two hours. The agency was eliminated in the first round.

Visuals

One of the most difficult things to master in giving presentations is learning how to work with, and from, your visuals. In a well-planned presentation your visuals can serve as notes. You should have visuals that give the key points as well as visuals that function as signposts. All of the material that you would normally have on notecards will probably be on your visuals. Your verbal discussion then becomes an elaboration of these visual "notes."

Both slides and boards can function as "notes" for the speaker. The main difference is that the lights are on with boards and the speaker is the primary focus of the audience's attention. With slides, the lights are down and the audience's attention shifts from the speaker to the screen. That's why the slides must be as dynamic—or more dynamic—than the speaker.

> Everyone should know how to operate all the equipment

EXHIBIT 6.4

WORKING FROM THE VISUALS

Good presenters work directly from the visual. This means:

1. You know what slide is coming next. If you are surprised by a slide, you lose credibility.

2. The minute a slide goes up, your audience's attention will be on the visual so you can also look to reassure yourself which slide it is.

3. As soon as a slide goes up, your audience will begin reading it. Either give them time to read or read it aloud and go from there. If you are saying something that is different from what is on the slide when it first goes up, their attention will be divided.

4. Talk about the visual that is up. Don't put the next visual up while you are concluding your last point. There should be total and immediate continuity between the visual and your words.

5. Don't read every word on every slide. Elaborate on what the slide says. If your slides are done properly all you need to do is fill in and round out. Since the eye reads silently more quickly than you speak, you'll automatically lose your audience if you try to read every visual.

6. Gesture toward the visual to help drive home the point and to keep the presentation animated.

7. Plan where you stand so you don't have to turn your back on the audience to read the visual.

8. Don't stand in front of the visual. Don't block the view of anyone in the audience.

Remember your audience is sitting there wondering if they should read or listen—most people can't do both at the same time. How you explain the visual leads them through this decision. Normally you read or paraphrase the visual with them, and then they listen while you explain. The visual is there to remind them of the key point you are developing.

If for some reason you can't use visuals—if, for example, the power goes out or you have to present on the run at an airport—then use words to help your audience visualize. If four reasons support a particular point, tell them, "there are four reasons why this makes sense. Reason number one is . . ." and continue to provide this visual structure to help them mentally see as well as hear your logic.

Props

The computer printouts and sample magazines mentioned earlier represent the kinds of props typically found in presentations. Anything you can bring in or mock up will make the presentation more interesting and help direct attention to your point.

If you are recommending store banners, brochures, a trade character or a point-of-purchase display, mock them up and display them. They will enliven the presentation and help people who can't imagine things visually. Showing them will help your audience understand what you are proposing, and will reduce the chance of misinterpretation.

Lecterns

A lectern is sometimes used in more formal presentations. Its use makes a statement, and to some people in the audience it can be intimidating. It may also act as a barrier between presenters and their audiences. Presenters like it, though, because it gives them a place to put their notes and something to hold on to if their knees start to buckle.

The more experienced people become, the less they need the security of a lectern. Don't hide behind the furniture. Experienced presenters usually prefer a more relaxed tone for their presentations. You can gradually wean yourself from a lectern with practice. When you come to a part of the presentation that you know really well, take a step or two toward the audience—or the screen if you are using visuals. You can also stand beside the lectern resting your arm on its side. This not only deformalizes your presentation, it is also good body language. It says, "I'm confident and in control."

Some presenters try to communicate being relaxed by leaning on a lectern with both hands or, even worse, placing their forearms on each side so that the audience can only see talking heads. If you stand behind a lectern, stand tall. Don't slouch. You can place one hand on the side, but gesture with the other. Guard against becoming part of the lectern. It's inanimate, dead wood.

Notes

Most experienced presenters don't write out their presentations word for word. If the presentation makes extensive use of visuals, they use these as their notes. The visuals point out the major sections, give the key points, and illustrate basic concepts. If you practice your section until you know it well, you can "talk" it through using visuals as your cue cards. Talk to the audience. Tell them about what you've done and how you came to the conclusion you are recommending. Know the material well, but don't memorize it.

Let your visuals be your notes

EXHIBIT 6.5

PROBLEMS WITH READING FROM NOTES

Why should a presentation *never* be read?

1. When you lower your eyes into a script, the audience lowers you into a hole six feet deep. You kill your animation and the presentation loses its life. You're dead.

2. A person reading from a script tends to fall into a monotone voice that can cure insomnia.

3. The words are no longer personal. The audience wonders who wrote them. Whose ideas are being presented?

4. You're wasting the audience's time. Since they can read just as well as you can, they will be asking themselves why you didn't just send them a copy and save them a trip to the meeting.

Good presenters can get by with using only the visuals as notes, but novice speakers may find that it is better to use notes than become confused. Also, the more technical the information, the more likely you will need notes.

Notes should be just that—notes. Just enough to cue your thoughts. Otherwise you will begin reading rather than speaking. And don't do anything with the notes that might detract from what you are saying. Don't shuffle or flash them.

If presentation boards are being used, you can write short notes with a soft lead pencil on the edge of the board. These cues should not be visible to people sitting in the front row.

Pointers

Pointers and circus barkers are out of place in most presentations

Use a pointer only if your visuals really require it. If you are showing maps, schematics, or large tables of numbers, a pointer may make sense. Otherwise it's merely a distraction. Most presenters play with it rather than point with it. The audience becomes more interested in what you are going to do next with the pointer than in what you are going to say next.

Try keeping one of those adjustable pen/pointers on the lectern. Only when you need to lead the audience through a complicated visual like a media flow chart will you really need the pointer. It is insulting to use it with a simple visual. When you do use a pointer, put it on the visual and hold it there. Don't wave it or tap in time with your delivery, and put it down as soon as you're done.

If you are in a darkened room, particularly a large one, the only kind of pointers you can use are flashlight or laser pointers. These require practice, as every little move becomes exaggerated and makes the light start dancing on the screen.

Other Stuff

Cigarettes have become unwelcome in most business situations so avoid them in presentations—chewing gum, likewise. Hands that are nervous sometimes play with things like paper clips, pencils, and keys. If yours do, put everything out of reach.

Avoid drinking from anything that is noisy such as a cup and saucer. A cup rattling on a saucer shows how nervous you are. You can spill a drink or knock it over—both disasters in presentations.

If you are speaking longer than 15 minutes, you may need water to keep your throat from getting dry. Put the water in a low glass, a coffee mug, or something that won't be easily knocked over.

When you need to take a drink, find a natural break and stop. Take your drink, then continue. No need to tell the audience you are thirsty or dry or anything else equally obvious. An audience will give a speaker personal time. If you need to wipe your forehead or mouth or blow your nose, just do it. By not commenting upon it, you'll call minimal attention to it and look more professional and self-confident.

PERFORMING AS A PROFESSIONAL

A presentation is a performance and the presenters are on stage. Personal style is important, as is a positive self-image. As a presenter you need to be able to read the room as well as read your notes. You're playing to an audience and the success of your message may depend upon how well you can analyze the message's effect and control the audience's attention. Performers have to be in control of other things, too, such as equipment and visuals, notes, and props. If you are prepared and manage the situation effectively, you will find yourself giving a polished performance.

CHAPTER 7

Delivering Your Message

KEY POINTS
✎ Expressiveness is expressed in your voice
✎ Body language: your presence should speak well for you
✎ Use videotape to see how your body talks
✎ Nerves can be good for you

VOICE

Your voice is one of your most important presentation tools. It's also one you have the least experience in consciously controlling. With practice and conscious effort you can control pitch, timbre, volume, speed, pauses, and pronunciation. You probably don't even realize how much you vary speed, pitch, and inflection in normal speech. That's what makes your language "expressive." In presenting you want to maintain that natural expressiveness—perhaps even accent it a little more. One copywriter concerned about his presenting abilities took acting lessons to learn proper breathing and vocal techniques.

Expressiveness is shown through your voice

HEARING YOURSELF AS OTHERS HEAR YOU

Most people don't hear themselves as others hear them. Even when you listen to yourself on an audio cassette or a videotape, you don't hear the voice on the tape the way you think you sound. That's because when you hear your voice from within your body, all the reverberations from your vocal track resonate in your ears. You may very well hear your own voice as richer and deeper than the one others hear from outside. That's why it's important to practice speaking using tape recordings. Spend a day with a tape recorder and you will meet a different you and get a better image of the true sound of your voice to others.

If you want your voice to sound to others like the voice you hear inside your head, you need to concentrate on pitch and timbre. Both are used to define meaning, and give emphasis and stress to your words.

VOCAL CHARACTERISTICS

Pitch

Pitch describes how high or low you speak and timbre reflects both volume and richness. When you talk, your voice just naturally flows up and down the scale. If it doesn't, you sound flat and monotonous. Your pitch should go down slightly at the end of major ideas or phrases. When it goes up at the end of a phrase, it sounds like you are asking a question and have not completed the thought. You leave the audience waiting for you to finish. On the other hand, if your pitch goes down too much at the end of a phrase, it sounds like you are fading off or are uninterested.

Your voice has a tremendous range of pitch that you can control. To do so, read a passage into a microphone and vary the pitch by speaking higher and lower, just like practicing scales. Listen to the tape recordings and try to find the voice that you hear in your mind when you speak. Practice at different levels until you have both the pitch at which you normally speak and the pitch you would like to hear locked into your mind. Achieving your preferred pitch level is simply a matter of hearing the difference and practicing.

Timbre

Manipulating timbre is harder. Rich voices are produced by people who speak with their vocal tracks "wide open." Tight, tiny, tinny and nasal voices come from vocal tracks that are "squeezed down." To experiment with varying timbre, stand upright, balanced comfortably on both feet. Push your shoulders back and tip your chin a little higher than you're normally used to. Physically, this "opens up" your voice box. When you stand hunched over with your shoulders forward and your chin down, you pinch your vocal track.

When you work on timbre, you're working on the source of your speech. Practice standing quietly and notice how you breathe. Are you breathing from your chest or your gut? Try inhaling first from your chest and then from your stomach. Can you feel the difference? Proper breathing makes a critical difference in speaking.

Put your hands on your waist with your fingers forward over your stomach muscles. Do you feel your muscles move in and out as you breathe? That's how you control timbre and volume in speaking. If you speak from your chest, your voice is likely to be tiny; if you speak from the gut, it's likely to be richer.

Actors and people who train with a voice coach will practice speaking like this until they have developed some control over the timbre of their voice. Timbre is like pitch—there is a range that you can control. Presentation speaking requires a rich, full-bodied voice, because it's considered warm, credible, and authoritative.

Volume

Volume is another aspect of your speaking voice that you need to study. Some people just naturally speak with a soft timid voice; others are loud and brash. In a small conference room, your normal speaking voice may be adequate, assuming it isn't pinched and tiny. In a larger room like a classroom, it is usually necessary to project. That means speaking louder—but actually when you "project," speaking louder means speaking more from the gut. Pull your voice up out of your shoes and project it, rather than yell.

It's better to be slightly on the loud side. This will ensure that everyone—even those in the back and those with some hearing problems can hear. Also, a voice that is louder than the normal speaking voice commands attention and is authoritative. Think about most commercial pilots' voices. When you hear a deep, rich and fairly loud voice saying, "This is your pilot speaking . . ." you generally feel more confident about the flight.

You may want to vary volume as a dramatic technique. If you consistently speak in a voice that's too soft to be heard, you may alienate your audience. You can, however, deliberately speak softer occasionally in order to control attention. People stop what they're doing and listen carefully in order to hear what someone is saying in a hushed voice. Likewise, when you occasionally raise your voice to make a point, you inevitably capture the listener's attention.

Dynamics are best practiced in the room you will be presenting in, since volume level varies with the size of the room and its acoustics. Experienced presenters can intuitively adjust volume. To work on your presentation style, try giving a section of your presentation in different rooms. Notice how the size and acoustic qualities of the rooms affect the sound of your voice. Practice adjusting your voice to create your desired inner voice image regardless of the room acoustics.

Many people let their voices drop when their minds begin to focus on the next part of the presentation. If you're thinking about something else and your voice trails off, the audience won't hear the end of your statement. Most points of emphasis fall at the end of a statement and if you habitually let your voice drop, you lose the opportunity to hammer home your point. To make sure this isn't your bad habit, tape record yourself making a presentation. Most people are totally unaware of this problem.

If you do have a problem with voice drop, practice thinking about emphasis. Force yourself to work out exaggerated ending points in order to keep your own attention on what you are doing. Then pause, turn to a visual and use it to collect your thoughts.

Speed

How fast you speak is a function of individual style. Some people are hyper and race through their material; others are slow and thoughtful, perhaps even plodding. Individual style is fine as long as it doesn't get in the way of your message.

If you speak too slowly or too fast, you will lose your audience. Generally we can listen faster than most people talk, but just because we can doesn't mean we're comfortable doing it. It's particularly exhausting if visuals are involved and we are processing information through both the visual and auditory channels. However, someone who talks slowly may be boring. Most people get impatient and let their minds race ahead of the speaker.

It is best to use a middle rate and then vary it to indicate mood. For example, when you're really excited about something, you tend to speak faster; when you're mulling over something you tend to speak slower. You can use those rate changes to cue the mood of different presentation sections.

Obviously you first need to determine your normal speaking rate. Tape record news and advertising announcers. Listen to the tapes for speaking rate and pacing. Identify a middle rate. Now tape record yourself talking on the phone as well as talking through a section of your presentation. Compare your phone conversation with your practice presentation and the tapes of the announcers. Practice talking into the mike until you feel you are approaching the "ideal" middle rate that you identified earlier. Practice at that rate until the basic tempo is locked into your mind.

Now, analyze your phone conversation. Do you always speak at the same rate? One reason presentations can seem so plodding is that the rate of speaking never changes. The presenter uses the same rate and other presenters may match it. Normally we are much more animated and our speaking rate varies with our topic. Do you vary the rates more in a phone conversation? Practice with two different sections of your presentation, one in which you want to appear thoughtful and one in which you want to project excitement. Tape record yourself again. Can you hear the difference in the moods you project?

Enunciation

Pronunciation is a very important part of speaking. If you don't say the words clearly, your audience simply won't get the message. Many people mumble when they speak. Their heads are down, they look at their feet, and they speak to the floor. Their mouths don't open wide enough to form the various word sounds. In the process the word sounds—particularly the beginnings and the endings of the words—get lost.

Poor enunciation is partly laziness but it is also directly related to projection and posture. If you are standing upright, shoulders back, and chin up, it's very difficult to mumble. Speaking rate is also a factor. If you are racing through your material, your words may get confused.

You can improve enunciation by practicing the techniques of projection and posture. If you speak fast, but you are working on slowing down the rate, then your enunciation also will improve. Once again, tape record yourself and listen to the sounds. Do you hear the beginnings and the endings of all your words?

In a videotape, look at your mouth. Does it open wide enough to form an *O*? Are the lips physically moving to form "plosives" like *P, B* and *D*? Run through the alphabet and notice how your lips and jaw move to make these letters. The same process is involved in making words, only it goes faster. As your enunciation speed picks up, don't cut down on the formation of letters.

Pauses

Good speakers use pauses as punctuation points. Pauses are permitted either before or after a major point. They are also used to signify a transition from one section to another or from one mood to another.

Pauses can be useful or they can be destructive. Someone who pauses frequently out of nervousness makes an audience uncomfortable. Saying "uhm" doesn't help fill the space—it just makes the pause more distracting. The problem is usually the opposite with novice presenters. There's a tendency to fill the air with sound and look upon a pause as a waste of a few valuable seconds.

Whenever you make a major point, it's a good idea to pause and let the idea "sink in." Don't just crash on to your next topic: give listeners a minute to reflect on the implications and rethink the logic. When you pause, look at your audience, particularly if you have said something extremely profound. A quiet stare says, "think about it."

When you are in a thoughtful part of the presentation, using pauses can help contribute to the reflective tone. When you are throwing a lot of data—like research findings—at the audience, let a pause give them time to absorb the numbers. During the question-and-answer period, pauses allow you to collect your thoughts and organize your answer.

BODY LANGUAGE

APPEARANCE COUNTS

Your presence should speak well for you

Your appearance involves a lot of dimensions—dress, poise, posture, gestures, facial expression, movement, and mannerisms. They all go together to make up the impression you give your audience. And they can all be used to communicate some aspect of your presentation message.

You want a presence that speaks well for you. You should be interested and interesting, vital, animated and enthusiastic. Get plenty of rest the night before and eat sparingly before you speak. Don't do anything which might dull your energy.

Dress

Dress is obviously an important factor in your audience's initial impression. You want to look successful, well-groomed, and faultlessly attired. It's hard to respect someone who is unkept.

Most of all you want to choose comfortable clothes that make you feel good. Don't wear anything that doesn't quite fit because you'll spend your time in front of the room pulling at it, adjusting it, and generally calling attention to your discomfort. If you are uncomfortable, you'll make your audience uncomfortable.

Business presentations usually call for business dress. Malloy's *Dress for Success* book details acceptable apparel for most business situations. You will probably find yourself most comfortable wearing something serious, professional, and conservative. For both men and women, that usually means the dark blue or grey suit—nothing that is flashy, too casual, or sexy. This is serious business, after all.

A presentation team may want to consider the effect of the team's appearance. Four people in contrasting plaid suits can be distracting. There may be a reason to plan some aspect of the dress to reinforce something related to the presentation—such as buttons or a particular color or style of tie. Be careful, however, with "costumed" dressing for a business presentation; it may come across as sophomoric. If you all show up in dark blue suits and maroon ties, your dress may be a distraction.

Expression and Eye Contact

After dress, the expression on your face is probably the next most important aspect of your appearance. Most business presenters try to be professional, yet warm and friendly.

A warm smile is usually appropriate. It projects good will. Furthermore, liking begets liking—if you want them to like you, you must signal that you like them.

Start with a smile

A tight jaw usually means someone is nervous, displeased, uptight, or angry. Before you go in the room, look in the mirror, loosen your jaw, relax your face, smile, and see if you can get some sparkle and warmth in your eyes. To do this run through some simple exercises actors use before going on stage. Move your head left and right as far as it will go and hold it there for five seconds. Now move your head up and down and hold it for five seconds in each extreme position. Massage your jaws. Press your tongue against the back of your bottom teeth. You should feel a pull in your voice box as you stretch those muscles.

Eye contact is an important part of addressing your audience. When you speak honestly to someone, you look them straight in the eyes. When you are embarrassed or trying to put something over on someone, you don't look them in the eyes. Consequently, to be believable in a business presentation, look directly at your audience. Don't look at the floor, the ceiling, or a distant wall. Develop a personal relationship with everyone in the room. Talk to each one directly, using eye contact to make them a part of your team. Most good presenters look around the room as they speak, stopping to look directly at various members of the audience. This is a way to move your thoughts around the room and keep everyone involved in the message development.

Looking at someone in a meeting for a length of time makes them feel like you are talking specifically to them. This can be flattering, and it also demands that they pay attention. You may want to use that technique with someone important like the department manager or CEO—the person who makes the ultimate decision. Because this technique commands attention, you shouldn't rely on it too much. Read the response of your listener and see if he or she appears to be flattered or irritated, and adjust accordingly. But don't overlook the junior members in the audience. They will be insulted if they notice you are playing to the big guys. It comes off as ingratiating.

How much eye contact is enough? How long should you look directly at one person? There are no set guidelines. The main criteria are, first, to establish and then to retain this feeling of "contact." As soon as the person you are looking at looks back, move on. This may take several seconds, or it may require only a glance. Eye contact is basically a way of saying "Are you with me?" Once you have your answer, go on and check with someone else.

Gestures

Gestures are best when they are spontaneous. If you have to think about them, they probably won't look natural. Old speech books are full of advice on cultivating gestural flourishes, most of which look inane when used before a live audience. The most natural place for your arms and hands is at your side. There's nothing wrong with that basic position.

The best gestures are natural

If you feel the need to practice gestures, do it as you practice in front of a mirror or videotape. In practice, however, overexaggerate all your gestures. Make them overly dramatic. Then, when you get in front of a live audience, forget all about gestures. Your body will remember the gestures, but in a more natural manner.

Don't repeat a motion so many times that it begins to attract attention to itself. Also avoid choppy, jerky motions from the elbow; the more natural gestures will use a loose swing of the entire arm from the shoulder. Equally problematic are gestures that end too soon. Hold the motion and allow time for the gesture to register. Jerky motions are a signal of nervousness.

Hands can have a mind of their own. Sometimes they want to help; sometimes they get in the way. Natural gestures are an important part of directing attention and emphasizing the points you make. In working with visuals on boards you have a natural focus for gestures, since you will be using your hands to demonstrate visually the relationships between the concepts.

Restless hands typically indicate that the speaker is nervous. They occupy themselves by jingling coins, playing with paperclips, folding and unfolding pieces of paper. These are distracting; they are also subconscious. The speaker probably doesn't even know he or she *has* nervous hands.

Sometimes hands gesticulate. They repeat one nervous gesture over and over. Messing with your hair, adjusting a necklace, or pushing glasses up on your nose can be distracting when the audience begins to notice the repetition.

To avoid these problems, videotape yourself giving a presentation. Watch your hands and see if they are nervous or gesticulating. Plan a counter behavior such as putting your hands in your jacket pocket or holding a pencil. If you are inclined to put your hands in your pockets, be sure to remove all coins and anything else with which you might play and make a distracting noise. Many presenters hold pencils or eyeglasses as a technique to keep them from some other nervous, distracting behavior.

If you don't have a lectern to hold on to, what should your hands do? Don't stick them in your pants pockets; don't click a ballpoint pen; don't play with a pointer. All of these draw the audience's attention and compete with the message. Either leave your hands at your sides or clasp them in front of you. (Don't put them in back unless you want to appear extremely pompous.) When your hands are clasped in front of you, they should be kept about waist high.

> Use a videotape to see how your body talks

Posture

An upright posture is physiologically important in order to control timbre and volume of speaking. But posture is also an important part of appearance. Moms have been prodding kids to ''stand up straight'' for so long that it seems redundant even to mention that posture is important in presentation. Videotape yourself; you may not even be aware that you slouch when you talk.

Some presenters have a carefully studied casual style about them. They can lean back against a table, hands in pockets, and talk with warmth and friendliness to any audience. But most people, particularly beginning presenters, are more comfortable in a formal mode. This demands, however, that you stand up straight with both feet firmly planted on the floor. Try not to hunch over a podium, leaning on it with your elbows for support. Don't give the impression that you are using a podium as a shield, as something to hide behind, or something to separate you from your audience.

When you are standing before an audience without a lectern in front of you, your feet should be shoulder width apart with your weight balanced equally. From this position you can step comfortably left, right, or straight ahead to make a point. This solid stance says you are confident of what you are saying, whereas putting your weight on one leg or rocking back and forth suggests vacillation.

Movement

The podium can be a speaking aid, but it can also be a trap. If you are too attached to the podium, you may appear rigid. To loosen up your tone and style, move away from the podium.

Movement, like your voice, can be used to emphasize things, or to indicate a change in pace or a change of sections in the presentation. Simply stepping to the side of the podium can indicate that you've moved from a formal report to a more personal discussion. Walking out in front of the podium or table makes the presentation more of a conversation and less of a speech.

Movement can also be used to focus attention. For example, if you wanted to use two presenters side by side, one could step forward a step when speaking just to indicate where audience attention is to be directed. When finished, that person steps back, and the other steps forward. The same technique can be used with two people presenting from one podium. These movements need to be subtle or they will look phony and contrived. They also need to be choreographed so people won't bump into each other.

Not all movements are good. Pacing is a nervous behavior that makes the audience uncomfortable. Balancing first on one foot and then the other is another indicator that you are unsure of yourself.

Use movement for emphasis

Analyzing

Body language is best analyzed with a videotape. Tape a rehearsal and then play the tape back with the sound off. You will be better able to see how your body "talks." Ask your colleagues to comment on what they see, too. It is difficult to analyze your own body language.

NERVOUSNESS

Everyone has it. Don't think you aren't a good presenter because you get nervous. Nervousness can be a positive when it gets you all charged up, or a negative when it conveys your fear and signals a lack of self-confidence. Political consultant Roger Ailes says, "They say that the bravest soldiers are often afraid in combat. Courage doesn't mean the absence of fear. It means fighting past fear and taking action." It's up to you to find that perfect balance where you can perform at your peak.

THE ROLE OF EXPERIENCE

There is no anti-nerves pill

The way to deal with nervousness is through experience. As Dale Carnegie said in his little book on public speaking, the only way to learn to swim is to get in the water. The more you present, the more you realize that being nervous isn't a disaster. And the more you present, the less nervous you will be. There is no anti-nerves pill; there is only anti-nervous practice. The only solution to nerves is to do it over and over.

Give presentations every chance you get. Take advantage of every opportunity in staff and group meetings to present to your colleagues. Work it out on your friends; then move to bosses, and finally to clients.

CHARACTERISTICS OF NERVOUSNESS

Shaking Hands

Hands that shake are one signal of nervousness. Gripping the podium until your knuckles turn white is not a successful solution. Above all, don't hold notes or a pencil—that just calls attention to something you wish would go away. A better solution is to clasp your hands in front of you or put them in your pockets. Try to do something physical with your hands—pick up a report, stack some books, pick up an exhibit or mock-up and point out features, or point to something on a map. Directed activity can sometimes overcome aimless shaking.

EXHIBIT 7.1

DEALING WITH NERVES

The main reason most people are nervous about presenting is that they are afraid they will do or say something that will make them look dumb or stupid. There are things you can do to reduce your nervousness.

1. Know what you are talking about. Really know the material. If there is an area you are sketchy on, don't be afraid to admit it.

2. Believe in what you are saying. If you are not convinced that the new creative is really best for your client, then either discuss it with your creative people until you are sold on it, or have someone else present it.

3. Don't be too hard on yourself. Think how you evaluate a presenter. If he or she fumbles over a word or loses his place, do you feel he or she is stupid—or just human?

4. Think of yourself as pumped up with adrenalin, not nerves. Look on nervousness as a positive.

Mannerisms

Someone with the potential to be a good presenter may have a personal style that is distracting—nervous tics, repetitive or forced gestures, continued use of ''uhm'' or phrases like ''you know.'' The solution once again is a videotape and lots of practice. Recognizing the problem is the first step. The solution may be as simple as just becoming conscious of the problem.

Mannerisms are a part of the nervous response to an uncomfortable, and possibly unknown, situation. It's part of the fight-or-flight response. To become comfortable presenting you have to make the situation less of a threat. That means practice. The more prepared you are, the less the unknown danger.

COPING WITH NERVOUSNESS

If a person doesn't know what to do with his or her hands, then maybe he or she can practice the controlled use of a pencil to deflect the internal discomfort. Simply holding a pencil or eyeglasses may occupy the hands enough to provide some feeling of security. On the other hand, someone who plays with a pencil until it becomes a distraction needs to learn never to present with a pencil anywhere nearby.

Common relaxation techniques can help. Breathe deeply before you get up to speak. Tighten and relax all the muscles you can think of—your hands, neck, shoulders, forehead, legs, and feet. Finally, remember that most signs of nervousness don't show; no one else may know you are nervous, so keep it your private little secret.

Most nervous presenters do a good job of hiding it. If you tell the audience you are nervous, they will start looking for signs. ''Is he perspiring, are his hands shaking, his knees wobbly?'' Their attention will be focused on your nervousness rather than on what you are saying.

The best way to cope with nervousness is to see it as something positive. Don't think of yourself as someone who is nervous. See yourself as a person who is all pumped up with adrenaline and ready to give an all-star performance!

CHAPTER 8

Presentation Follow-Up

KEY POINTS

- ✎ Anticipate the questions
- ✎ Practice your answers
- ✎ Survive dogfights
- ✎ End on a social note
- ✎ Don't forget the housekeeping chores
- ✎ Leave something with them as a reminder
- ✎ Get together afterwards and talk it over
- ✎ Rely on plansbook for details

HANDLING Q & A

How you handle questions and answers after the presentation is completed may have more impact than anything else. After all, Q & A comes at the end and is most likely to be remembered.

ATTITUDE

Attitude is everything. Don't be defensive. Consider the Q&A just another chance to explain. Clarification is often needed, and it has nothing to do with the quality of your presentation.

You can disarm the audience by presenting a warm, positive attitude during Q&A. In response, questions may be less pointed. Another good disarming technique is to open the Q&A session by leading with one of your own questions. This can be a question directed to the client or directed back to your own team members.

ANTICIPATE

Plan your Q&A session just like you plan the presentation. Anticipate every possible question. Work with your colleagues at the office and anyone else you can get to listen to your presentation and develop a question bank. Ask "harpooners," the ones who try to pin you to the wall, to be your surrogate client. Tell them to ask you every difficult question they can think of. Ask, in particular, for the "dumb" questions because those are the ones that will most likely trip you up. If you know there are sensitive areas or areas of disagreement in the presentation then structure a whole series of answers to extend your justification for this recommendation. Consider it just one more chance to hit them again with more rationale.

Put your "harpooners" to work

Some presentations have been deliberately scripted with "holes" designed to stimulate questions. If the client picks up on that area, you have another supporting argument ready to deliver.

Difficult Questions

Some situations are just naturally hard to handle—the client dumps on you, you find yourself digging one ditch after another, or the whole team gets caught up in a dogfight.

If it appears that the question is personal, perhaps an attack on you or your team, try to find a way to depersonalize it. Find something in the question that relates to the message you presented and try to focus attention back in that direction. Don't lose your cool. Train the team to let the key presenter or someone else who is adept at thinking on his or her feet handle the questions.

Don't take difficult questions personally

Don't take it personally. John Grant warns that it's absolutely critical that no one on the team fall into this, particularly creative people who tend to have problems with the ownership of the idea. Don't let it become a personal attack; move it around to someone else on the team. Grant suggests you focus on the logic, not the emotion. Make your response logical.

Loaded questions can be used to trip you up. Sometimes they have a hidden agenda. You know it's there but you don't know what it's about. See if you can turn it back on them. Ask them to rephrase the question or ask them, "what do you think . . . what was your experience?" Probe for more information so you can find the mine field before answering.

EXHIBIT 8.1

HANDLING Q & A

Here are some more ideas on how to handle Q & A.

1. Relax, laugh, smile.
2. Avoid lengthy answers.
3. Think before answering. Don't just blurt something out. A pause is Okay.
4. Rephrase the question to make sure you understood it.
5. Ask them to rephrase to verify that you heard the question correctly.
6. Paraphrase something you said before. Have several ways to state every argument, every point.
7. If you need to buy time, ask the rest of the team (or the client) how they feel about it.
8. Don't answer something they didn't ask.
9. Designate someone to field the questions—that gives you time to think and someone else to summarize what you've said in case you were incomplete or unclear.
10. Don't bluff. If you don't know, say so. Say you'll get back with the information—and follow through.
11. Separate shotgun questions into pieces and answer them piece by piece.
12. Allow the questioner to finish his/her sentence even if he/she interrupted you.
13. Look directly at the person asking the question otherwise he/she may think you are not listening or do not think the question is important.
14. Be sure to answer questions from all sections of the room.
15. Don't use phrases like, ''Frankly,'' or ''To be honest with you.'' They give the impression that you haven't been honest up to that point.
16. Don't say one person's name unless you are prepared to call everyone by name.

Some people are quibblers. They like to argue and they will find some point to debate regardless of its insignificance. What they want is recognition, so give it to them. Respond with something like, ''good point . . . I'm glad you noticed that.'' If they go on and on, you can deflect them by suggesting that you talk about it after the meeting.

Some people are just plain hostile. If this becomes disruptive, then sometimes the only solution is to invite him or her to get it out. Sit still while the venom flows; get it out on the table. Respond by saying first that you respect his or her view. See if you can find any point of agreement and focus on it. A turnaround technique might work if you can find some question to use in response that demands a positive response.

During Q&A you will run up against debaters, windbags, the confused, and people with axes to grind. Prepare for them ahead of time so their behavior doesn't come as a shock. Have a friend act out a role as a shark or barracuda so you can practice dealing with hostility or incoherence. You must be pleasant, helpful, concerned and in control. In most of these situations you'll find that the rest of the audience is on your side.

Thinking on Your Feet

The secret to thinking on your feet is preparation and flexibility. Know what you are up against, psych out the confrontations and conflicts, and anticipate the questions. Skill in reading the room and handling hot potatoes comes from experience, so the best preparation is practice. Lean on your friends and colleagues and tell them to ask you the dumbest and the toughest questions they can come up with. That's how you learn to think on your feet.

PRACTICE AN ENDING

The problem with having the Q&A session at the end is that you turn this prime time over to the audience. If they introduce opposition or irrelevant points, you have lost ground that you may have been building very carefully for the last 30 minutes. For this reason some presenters prefer to have the questions during the presentation, although many people feel that these questions make it even harder to keep the logic on track with distractions coming in from the right and left.

One solution is to write and practice an ending for the Q&A session. Use it to restate your key points once again. If you are a flexible thinker, you can prepare the ending, but leave it open enough so you can tie it into some of the more significant questions raised during Q&A. This closing is your last chance to dynamite through the dust.

WHEN THE MUSIC STOPS

There's a tendency to deflate the minute the presentation is over. But don't just sink into the nearest chair and start pulling off your shoes. Unfortunately, there are usually more duties to be handled, and sometimes there are still more events and people to meet.

SOCIALIZING

Frequently the official presentation may be followed with a social gathering like a reception. This can be used to pull everyone together, build camaraderie, and downplay any residual us vs. them thinking. Furthermore, it's a chance for more informal feedback from everyone—particularly from those who didn't speak up during the official presentation time.

CLEAN-UP DUTY

Don't forget that someone has to put away the equipment, load up the visuals, and restore the room to its original arrangement. The stage manager may miss the party, but it's an essential duty.

LEAVE-BEHINDS

Leave-behinds are like your calling card

You may want to prepare a "leave-behind" for the client representatives. Hand-outs and other leave-behind materials refresh the client's memory regarding your presentation. Ten hours after you present the client may only remember about 20 percent of what you said and certainly would have a hard time repeating it to colleagues without such aids. Copies of creative executions are fairly standard, as are research findings. A timetable is a useful prod for decision making. Execution summaries are useful both in the beginning to let the client representatives know where the presentation is headed, and at the end as a leave-behind.

Tom Hagan suggests that you give these leave-behinds a lot of thought. In a competitive new business presentation, this leave-behind is like your calling card. Hagan suggests you analyze it in terms of your competition. "Anticipate them," he says. "Remember, your competition knows you, so confound them by doing something different than what they might expect." John Grant, for example, has used audio tapes as leave-behinds. He uses them not only to remind clients of advertising jingles he has created, but to allow clients to replay key points.

A variation on the leave-behind is a follow-up letter. This might summarize the strengths of your proposal, but it should also summarize the reasons why your agency should be chosen. Make sure your highlights are really highlighted.

Grant remembers an innovative technique used by an agency, Brock & Associates, with which he worked. After pitching a restaurant chain named Le Peeps, the agency every day sent the chain one in a series of small, framed lithographs. The little pictures showed an egg opening up a crack at a time. The last one in the series showed a little chicken peeping out and saying, "Brock."

THE PLANSBOOK

While some kind of leave-behind is appropriate for most presentations, in major advertising campaign presentations, the presentation is summarized in a written document called a plansbook. The book may be given to the client either before or after the presentation.

While the focus of this book is on presentations, the plansbook is an important companion document. This book should be planned at the same time as the presentation. It contains all the details of the recommendations as well as the supporting justification. It is a confidential document that puts the promises in writing.

The book is intended to be a reference. Everything that is in the presentation is also covered in the book, but in greater depth. The presentation focuses on the highlights of the recommendations, paying careful attention to the logic and justification of the key proposals. The book provides the details, explanation, and documentation.

Because it contains massive amounts of information, the book should be well-organized. A good contents page is essential; indexing helps. The tone is usually friendly but, as one agency executive points out, "it should be the kind of communication your audience likes. And you had better find that out ahead of time."

The book is usually designed to look like the presentation, with similar graphics on the cover and inside on the sectional pages. Both the book and the presentation visuals establish the identity of the team or firm making the presentation. This graphic image needs strong continuity to tie the book to the presentation.

Most of all, the book and written materials have to be perfect; spelling, grammar, and reproduction should be flawless. Hagan explains, "It should reflect the kind of work the client can expect in the future."

DEBRIEFING

Debriefing is an important part of the post-presentation schedule. It's a good idea to sit down after every presentation, or even practice, and talk through it while it is still fresh. What kinds of problems cropped up? Was any section too complex? Did everyone emphasize the right things? Did anyone say anything that didn't feel right? Were there any clunkers? If this presentation is to be repeated, what needs to be changed?

PRESENTATION EVALUATION

There are two primary ways to improve your presentation skills. First, learn all you can about the fundamentals of making a good presentation. Second, get feedback from your audience. Without audience feedback, you merely practice and entrench bad habits.

Perfecting presentation skills is a process of trial and error. What works with one audience at one time on a particular subject may not work under different circumstances. Therefore, after each presentation you give, you should ask the audience to evaluate three areas: the presentation organization and technique, the presentation content, and you as a presenter.

Generally, a successful presentation must score high in all three of these areas. When a presentation is "lost," you should find out which one was weak. Don't accept the general brushoff, "We just didn't like your idea." Find out why. Consider these reasons:

- It was short on support

- It didn't sound logical

- It was unclear—the audience didn't understand what you were saying

- The audience wasn't convinced of the recommendation's value

- The audience's attention drifted, so it missed some of the information presented

While you want to get a good handle on what went wrong during your presentation, you should also find out what worked. Too often, critiques focus only on negatives. Consequently, the good points are not reinforced and are soon forgotten.

Remember, presentations are one of the ways upper management gets to know its people, especially those at the junior level. While they may not always agree with your recommendations, they should always be impressed with you. Feedback gives you a chance to make an even better impression every time you present.

Indirect Audience Feedback

One way to understand your presentation's impact on the audience members is to spend some time reviewing their behavior. First, judge the overall attentiveness of your audience during the presentation. Were they interested and engaged by your remarks? Second, review the questions asked during and after the presentation. Then ask yourself a few:

- Were questions concentrated on a specific point or section? You may not have explained that section sufficiently.

- Were questions aggressive and challenging? If so, the audience may have taken an adversary stance.

- Were they asking for clarification of things you had explained? Perhaps they failed to hear them because they had lost interest.

- Did questions prompt more questions? Maybe you weren't prepared to answer clearly and completely.

Finally, observe what the audience said and did after the presentation ended. Did they talk about what you said, or everything else but? Did more than three or four say ''good job'' and mean it? Did audience members purposefully avoid you, or did they search you out to talk about your topic? By answering these questions, you can draw some valuable conclusions about your effectiveness—or lack thereof.

Direct Audience Feedback

You can get direct audience feedback by videotaping or audio taping your presentation, and by using audience critique forms.

You get the best feedback when you videotape your presentation. While this isn't always possible—sometimes it's too expensive, and it isn't appropriate during a new business pitch—you should do it whenever you can. A videotape will accurately report:

- What you said

- How you said it

- What your body language said

- How you responded to questions

- Whether you pulled your ear, slouched on the lectern, stood in front of your visuals, etc.

While audio feedback isn't as complete as it is with video, audio taping your presentation is much easier and less expensive. Done discreetly, it can even capture a new business pitch. Have one of your staff run the recorder, or place one inside the lectern before the presentation begins. Don't be obvious about carrying one up with you, or the audience may think you are just practicing on them.

Audience critique forms can also gather feedback. Once again, this is not always appropriate, but it should be done whenever possible.

The type of critique form you use depends on you, your presentation, and your subject. Questions can be open-ended, like ''What did you like about the presentation? What did you think was the main message? What things in the presentation could have been better?'' Questions can also be more structured. For example, you can ask the audience to rate, on a five- or seven-point scale, to what extent they agree or disagree with statements like ''The presentation was interesting and kept my attention'' and ''The presentation made good use of audiovisuals.'' The critique form should follow the rules used to design questionnaires. Don't use leading questions, and address only one idea in each question.

Critique forms should be kept fairly short and simple. Keep in mind that the people filling them out are doing you a favor. In presentations to more than 50, you may want only a few people to complete the critique. You don't need everyone's opinion. If at all possible collect the forms before people leave or, chances are, you will never receive them.

Coping with Criticism

Don't forget that when most people critique, they emphasize the negative. Be prepared to have your ego assaulted. Don't let the critique forms discourage you. The audience may forget to mention all the good things you did—and they are probably comparing you to the best presentations they have ever heard or seen.

Defensiveness is a natural reaction to negative comments. But don't try to explain away the criticism. Rather, try to determine what prompted the comments and then build your next presentation with those comments in mind.

Keep critique forms short and simple

WRAPPING IT UP

Presentations vary greatly. They vary in level of formality, size of audience, function and purpose, audiovisual use, and expense. Once you understand that and can plot where your presentation falls in the scheme of things, then you're ready to begin planning your own winning presentation.

However, planning doesn't stop with the presentation. Make sure your plan includes all the wrap-up activities. A special social event, like a reception, has its own set of arrangements to be handled. Plan for a leave-behind or a follow-up letter. Don't forget the housekeeping clean-up chores. And schedule a debriefing session as soon after the presentation as is feasible. The wrap-up details may be just as important to your success as the presentation itself.

APPENDIX

PLANNING CARDS

Visual:

Key Point:

Support:

Visual:

Key Point:

Support:

SLIDE PLANNER

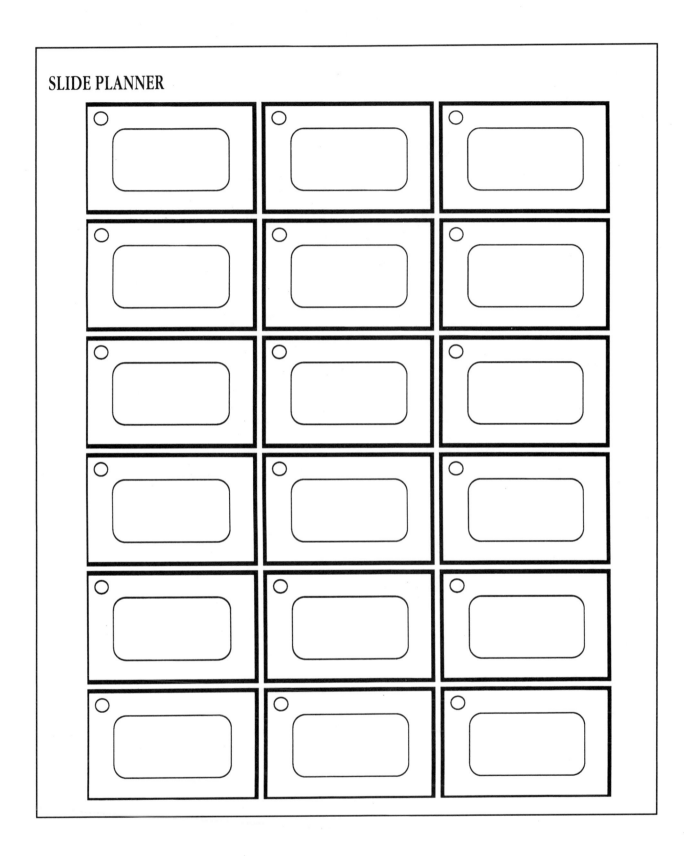

STORYBOARD FORMAT

Audio:

Audio:

Audio:

Audio:

SLIDE STORYBOARD FORMAT

MASTER PRESENTATION CHECKLIST

THE PRESENTATION COMPONENTS:

_____ the slides (already in trays)

_____ the boards

_____ a layout pad

_____ the videotape

_____ the audio tape

_____ the overhead transparencies

_____ handouts, leave-behinds

_____ plansbooks

_____ props

THE ROOM CHECK:

_____ light switches and light sources

_____ outlets

_____ projection screen

_____ blackboard

_____ write-on/wipe-off boards

_____ bulletin boards

_____ speakers, sound system

_____ tables and chairs (how arranged?)

_____ lectern

_____ heating and air-conditioning controls

_____ ventilation, windows and how they open

DRESSING THE ROOM:

_____ name tags or cards

_____ team roster

_____ notepads

_____ pencils, markers, or pens

_____ coffee

_____ cups

_____ sweetener, creamer, stirrers

_____ napkins

_____ rolls, donuts, cookies

_____ soft drinks

_____ water jug and glasses

OTHER THINGS YOU MAY NEED TO BRING:

_____ slide projector/s

_____ slide projector stand (preferably with adjustable legs)

_____ dissolve

_____ zoom lens

_____ projector rack (holds multiple projectors and dissolve unit)

_____ remote control and extension for the remote

_____ overhead projector

_____ $3/4''$ video equipment: monitor, VCR player

_____ $1/2''$ video equipment: monitor, VCR player

_____ projection screen

_____ audio cassette player

_____ easel with tray

_____ easel with pad mount (Check easel—does it have removable tray, pegs? Are all the pieces there?)

_____ portable bulletin board

_____ lectern

_____ pointer, light pen

EMERGENCY SUPPLIES:

_____ projector bulbs

_____ spot lights

_____ podium light

_____ masking tape

_____ transparent tape

_____ duct tape

_____ black electrical tape

_____ push pins

_____ extension cords

_____ strip outlet

_____ adaptor plugs

_____ chalk

_____ felt tip markers

_____ markers for transparencies

_____ dry erase markers

CONTACTS:

room arrangements/reservation _____

technical person for room _____

A-V technician _____

REFERENCES

Roger Ailes. "Even Heroes Get Scared." *Management Digest.*

Dennis Becker. "The Big Pitch: Sales Presentations." *Presentations.* February 1994.

Steve Bergsman. "Marketing Presentations—Finding the Balance." *Journal of Property Management.* November 1993.

Dale Carnegie. *How to Develop Self-Confidence and Influence People by Public Speaking.* New York: Pocket Books, 1956.

William M. Claggett. "How Clients View Pitches." *Advertising Age.* October 19, 1987, p. 18.

Stuart Elliot. "Sears Is Reviewing Part of its Merchandise Account." *The New York Times.* January 25, 1993.

Greg Farrell. "The Biggest Call of All." *ADWEEK.* December 6, 1993.

Debra Goldman. "Wild Pitch." *ADWEEK.* September 28, 1992.

Debra Goldman. "Think Small." *ADWEEK.* November 15, 1993.

Paul S. Hirt. *Newspaper Presentations.* Chicago: National Newspaper Promotion Association, 1964.

Ron Hoff. "What's Your Presentation Quotient?" *Advertising Age.* January 16, 1978, p. 93.

Nigel Holmes. *Designer's Guide to Creating Charts and Diagrams.* New York: Watson-Guptill Publications, 1984.

Richard Kern. "Making Visual Aids Work for You." *Sales & Marketing Management.* February 1989.

Thomas Leech. *How to Prepare, Stage and Deliver Winning Presentations.* New York: American Management Association, 1982.

John Malloy. *Dress for Success.* New York: Warner Books, 1978.

Leonard F. Meuse, Jr. *Mastering the Business and Technical Presentation.* Boston: CBI Publishing Co., 1980.

Nancy Millman. "30-Second Ads Agency's Reward for Months of Work." *Chicago Tribune.* March 28, 1993.

George L. Morrisey. *Effective Business and Technical Presentations.* Reading, Mass.: Addison-Wesley, 1968.

LaTresa Pearson. "Multimedia Hits the Road." *Presentations.* November 1993.

LaTresa Pearson. "Releasing the Power." *Presentations.* February 1994.

Joel Raphaelson. "Winning a Prestigious Local Account Against 44 Other Agencies." *Viewpoint.* April/May 1992.

Randall Rothenberg. "Seducing These Men." *The New York Times.* October 20, 1991.

"SalesTalk." *Sales & Marketing Management.* May 1989.

Gerald Schorin. "Notes on Advertising Presentations." An unpublished paper. Michigan State University, 1982.

John Sculley with John A. Byrne. *Odyssey: Pepsi to Apple . . . A Journey of Adventure, Ideas and the Future.* New York: Harper & Row, 1987.

Thayer C. Taylor. "Show and Tell that Sells." *Sales & Marketing Management.* April 1990.

Susanne G. Townsend. "Presenting 11 Ways to Catch Their Eye." *Advertising Age.* October 22, 1984.

Larry Tuck. "Medical Provider Scales Back High-Tech Presentations." *Presentations.* February 1994.

INDEX